9/98

Start Your Own ZINE

A JET LAMBERT GUMPTION GUIDE

Everything you need
to know to put
it into print!

Start Your Own ZINE

A JET LAMBERT GUMPTION GUIDE

by
Veronika Kalmar

HYPERION
New York

ISBN 0-7868-8217-4

Designer: Stewart Williams
Art Director: Simon Sung
becker&mayer! Editor: Jennifer Worick
Hyperion Editor: Lisa Jenner Hudson
Hyperion Production Editor: David Lott

Produced by becker&mayer!, Ltd.

FIRST EDITION

10 9 8 7 6 5 4 3 2 1

This book is dedicated to my parents, Laszlo and Marlis, for teaching me how to think for myself.

Acknowledgments

Thanks to the following people for their input, support, and at times endless patience.

Jim Becker

Breean Beggs

Jenny Bendel

Carla DeSantis

Karen Gerwin-Stoopack

Jeff Gilbert

Lisa J. Hudson

Kathy Kochler

Wendy Stadish

Wendy Weisberg

Jennifer Worick

and everyone who has ever created a zine.

Special thanks to

Buzzy

Mike C.

Nancy Ostrander

J.R.

Barbara Rodriguez

Cynthia Rose

Smitty

Jason Sutherland

The Hellabitches

Steve Tudor

CONTENTS

FOREWORD

by Carla DeSantis,
Publisher of ROCKRGRL

Everyone at one time or another has a burning idea or obsession they would like to share with a sympathetic and like-minded audience. Thanks to constantly evolving computer technology and simple-to-use publishing software, anyone with a pen and paper and a little time on his or her hands now has an opportunity to be seen and heard by multitudes of people by creating his or her very own zine.

Covering a wide variety of topics from the very personal to the world political, zines are in a class of their own. They range in design from the trendy photocopied look to full color throughout. Big, small, radical, sentimental, or about nothing in particular, one of the most compelling things about zines is that there are absolutely no rules, except the ones the editor makes up as he or she goes along. In fact, zines no longer have to conform to the archaic ideas of print. E-zines—computer-generated magazines that exist solely on-line— are giving small publishers even more outlets to self-expression.

Of course, carving your own niche requires some mighty hefty tools, and a budding zine entrepreneur faces many of the same challenges of any other business person.

The idea to turn my own personal obsession into a zine came about in the summer of 1994. I had been catching up on reading the latest rock and roll magazines, and discovered that the way my colleagues (women musicians) were portrayed in the rock media made me ill. After discussing my disgust for months with others who shared my opinion, I decided to throw caution to the wind and my hat into the ring. *ROCKRGRL,* a zine for and about women in the music industry, was born.

Unfortunately—and like most people who publish zines—I was big on ideas and short on experience and cash. I didn't realize that my ambitious bimonthly schedule was a much taller order than I ever could have anticipated. I figured my writing experience and public relations background would come in handy, but I didn't know the first thing about advertising or printing or distribution or word counts. Once I had my beautiful first issue in hand, I was shocked to find out how much postage for the final product was going to cost. I often relied upon the kind advice of other zine publishers when things got too confusing. Two and a half years later, I have a much better handle on things. I understand how distribution works and how to attract advertisers. I know a bit more about the printing process. And I'm aware of my postage costs.

I wish this book had been available when I first decided to do a zine. It would certainly have made a huge difference in the evolution of *ROCKRGRL*. Most people decide to do a zine because it sounds like fun. That certainly is true. Sharing your passion with the world is one of the most rewarding things a person can do. But it is a lot of work. There are many hidden issues to deal with. Sometimes it's just choosing the right glue-stick. Other times you might find yourself dealing with editorial content that could result in a lawsuit.

Freedom of the press is not meant to be a forum to slander or defame anyone else's character. Because most zine publishers don't have a fact-checking department or the deep pockets needed to stave off litigation, this can often be an extremely sticky situation. When you use writers other than yourself, you must be especially cautious about this. In the music business, it's very common to hear artists claim, "So and so ripped me off." Are you prepared to deal with a lawsuit from "so and so" if there's no merit to the claim? As a publisher, you are fully responsible for everything that is printed in your zine.

I am continually amazed by the feedback I get from *ROCKR-GRL* readers. While the vast majority are glowing and positive ("Keep up the good work!"), there are always a few exceptions. The honeymoon period between new zine and reader can be very brief. Also, as a former musician, I was used to getting an instant reaction from an audience, so I found the first few months when I didn't receive reader mail frustrating. I could not gauge whether or not I was succeeding in presenting the articles in an interesting and informative way.

This book is designed to help you navigate your way through the zine maze. Those of us who have done this before have learned the hard way that there's a whole lot more to publishing than just hav-

FOREWORD

ing this great idea. Bringing an idea to fruition is always a challenge. But with this book and a little homework, publishing a zine can provide the ultimate form of self expression—after all, *Rolling Stone* was once a zine, too.

Good luck!

—Carla DeSantis

THE EVOLUTION OF A REVOLUTION

BEGINNINGS 1400-1900

Blame the whole glorious mess on Johann Gutenberg. He invented the printing press in 1454 and unwittingly started the independence of thought which led to zines (also called fanzines). Gutenberg used his creation to print the Bible, thus allowing people to interpret the good book for themselves. It didn't take long for the powers that be to note how much power the mass distribution of printed information had, and the thought police jumped quickly into action. The war has been raging ever since—in one form or another. In England, printers had to fight for the right simply to publish during the 1700s; and a century-long battle for the right to criticize followed after that. Those clashes led to the "forceful journalism" practiced during the American Revolution and the early years of the new nation. Rather than the supposedly unbiased standard used in the mass media today, papers then were published openly assuming a specific political or social viewpoint—much like zines today. Early American publishers expected that their readers possessed the smarts to determine *which truth* best fit them. Simultaneously, there were papers dedicated to trade. Commerce was their purpose, and they were free from political or social leanings.

Early publishers were also printers. But eventually the power of disseminating ideas through publishing transferred to those possessing the financial means to purchase printing, and through that, public opinion. In the era of the Penny Press, between 1833 and 1837, advertising and media merged. Ignoring social responsibility, these papers reported lurid details of crime and pestilence for the sake of increasing circulation to satisfy their advertisers. They were the forerunners of the modern newspaper and, ironically, led to the rise of investigative reporting.

During these transformations there was always self-publishing, although such excursions were done primarily for political or religious reasons. Obviously, individual thought did not perish. It was, however, limited to the published works of philosophers such as Nietzsche and Kierkegaard, or transmitted through the now-lost art of letter writing.

One modern exception was the Dadaists in Europe and New York—the parents of Surrealism. They self-published solely for the amusement of tweaking the institutions of the time. It's no wonder Dadaists created the publications most similar to modern zines. Both movements—Dadaism (which existed from the late teens of this century to the early 1920s) and Punk (from which zines sprang)—share common elements. First, outsiders consider them nihilistic, but—more important—both employ unrestrained, impromptu expression to jolt an audience into awareness, if not thought.

It took modern technology and the popularization of the mimeograph process in the 1950s for self-publishing to become available to the masses. Something like the copy machines of today, mimeograph machines involve a cylinder. But the "originals" were stencils, mounted page-by-page on the cylinder; ink forced through the letters stamped out duplicates quickly, and allowed people to produce copies inexpensively. This way, writers-as-publishers reclaimed printing, if only to a minimal extent. Mimeo was used primarily by the Beats to distribute small literary magazines.

THE 1970s

The combination of Punk and the popularization of the copy machine—both of which took place in the 1970s—launched zines and alternative publishing as we know them today. Suddenly anyone could publish a "magazine" about whatever they had in mind. And they did.

The DIY (Do It Yourself) ethic led to whole pockets of self-published zines. "Fanzines," as they were then known, tossed aside all pretenses to journalistic objectivity and were highly opinionated publications revolving around music, politics, and freedom from commercial oppression. Early fanzines featured crudely hand-drawn or photocopied photographs on their covers. Internally, they consisted of photocopied pages of typed or handwritten copy, more shadowy photographs, and cut-and-paste graphics stolen from other sources. Advertising, often free or in trade, also provided visuals.

THE 1980s

Until recently, copyright has been of little concern to zines. Throughout the '80s zine publishers freely stole the art they used to mock society. No one cared because those who might take offense never saw the results. A favorite target for send-up was the traditional '50s and '60s family and the images that depicted it—not to mention the scrumptious food they ate, like Jell-O salads and Spam. But the increased awareness of zines did result in one unfortunate problem: along with more readers and larger circulations came mainstream exposure and lawsuits. Now some zines even copyright their own material.

The '80s also saw the rise of *Factsheet Five,* a zine dedicated to reviewing other zines. It provided the first central source for finding out about and ordering zines. In the music field, zines were first distributed to record stores by independent record labels during that decade. Catalogs and of course word-of-mouth became the main ways people tracked down zines, and newsstands began to create room on their overstocked shelves for select self-publishers.

THE 1990s

The desktop publishing boom of the '90s narrowed the visual difference (sometimes gap) between magazines and zines, making zines more appealing to retailers. And since stores displayed an interest, magazine distributors opened their doors to zines. Additionally, distributors and small shops dedicated strictly to zines emerged and the rise of e-zines not only opened up a free flow of information, but created a whole new area of law.

Although zines were born during the Punk scene, the expansion of media conglomerates has facilitated their continued growth. Zines serve and provide an outlet for the subcultures of society not served by mainstream media: *Fat Girl* caters to obese lesbians, while *Thrift Score* celebrates the joys of secondhand shopping. Additionally, *Out West* celebrates the road trip and *Murder Can Be Fun* examines the darker side of true crime.

GO FORTH AND PUBLISH

Zines produce erratic, erotic, and controversial literature. They also provide strikingly uninhibited analyses of popular culture and society—yours! Free from the restraints that dog traditional media, they can tantalize the minds of those in emerging and peculiar cultures. The possibilities are endless. Just fill in the gaps. If you're interested, so is someone else. Publish!

CHAPTER ONE
ACCESS AND INTERVIEWS

What is access and why do you need it? Access is getting to talk to people, and so the importance of access varies greatly depending on what you want to do with your zine. If your publication is dedicated to an obsession with collecting electrical line insulators, chances are access will not be a big problem. You will probably be writing about the history behind specific types of insulators and other collectors will be more than happy to chat about their assortment of colored glass. On the other hand, if your zine focuses on international politics, you might find access to the key players in that arena a tad more difficult. Luckily, most zines that rely on interviews are based on some aspect of popular culture, and those interviews are easy to arrange.

This chapter focuses on how to gain access to the people you want to talk to, whether through formal channels like publicists, or through informal means like letters (snail mail) or on the Internet. It will also provide basic pointers on how to prepare for and conduct a successful interview.

AIM HIGH, BUT HAVE A BACKUP PLAN

If you want to exorcise your childhood demon of talking to exercise guru Jack LaLanne, try it. Just make sure you have an interview with the woman who lives two blocks down the street and recently published a book on Facercise in case the LaLanne story falls through. How do you get the LaLanne interview? The same way you track down any interview. The first step is to find the publicity department.

- Look for a book, record, video, or other piece of merchandise produced by that person, and locate the name of the company that released it.
- Call directory information in either Los Angeles or New York first and ask for the company number. Chances are you'll find it.

- If the company is not listed in these cities, try a business directory at the public library. Yes, it may take some digging, but eventually you'll locate the company's phone number.
- Give them a call and ask for the publicity department.
- If you're covering a particular industry, it pays to invest in a directory which lists major contacts. It might not provide the exact number, but with persistent questions and telephone calls, you will find the right person.

The publicist may talk to you, or he or she may not. Truth is, the larger the circulation of your zine—a number a publicist will ask for along with a copy of your publication—the more likely you'll get access. You probably won't nail that Jack LaLanne interview the first time around, but after receiving repeated phone calls and numerous copies of your ultra-cool zine, a particular publicist might remember your name, send you a product, and grant a future request. One point to remember is not to pester your friendly publicist on a daily basis—they have *lots* of folks to talk to.

"Zines usually aren't that pesky," says Wendy Weisberg, associate director of West Coast publicity for Virgin Records. "If I tell you we don't have press dates organized, and I'll call you as soon as I am aware of the dates, you should trust me on that. You shouldn't have to call me. But sometimes publicists need a reminder. If you haven't heard back from them, call two weeks after your initial contact."

ESTABLISH CONTACTS

The ability to get interviews relies on having contacts. Basically, a contact is someone who can provide you with access and trusts you enough to let you have it. It makes sense that you'll have better access if you establish a relationship with the publicists who handle the people you are interested in *before* you ask them to set up an interview. If he or she knows your approach and philosophy, a publicist will feel more at ease providing you with access to someone he or she considers important. First, however, you have to track those publicists down. To find the publicists who promote the people or items you're interested in:

- Make a list of subjects and people you wish to cover.
- Call the appropriate offices and ask who handles what you cover.
- Note the proper spelling of the publicist's name as well as his or her address!

- To save yourself time in the future, track these items in an address book.

Once you have established a relationship with a publicist at a certain organization, he or she can direct and recommend you to other publicists in the same company. That's a contact.

Here is how Weisberg prefers to be contacted: "I like someone to call me and say, 'Hi, I'm starting a zine.' Then I'll ask a few questions like, 'How often do you publish? Is it going to be a color cover? What area are you from? How many pages is it going to be, and what is the focus?' And I like to know what's up with advertising because if people call and they don't have a game plan, it seems like they might just be after a few free records . . . but I'm not the sort of person who says I will only send you records for review after your first issue. If people make an articulate appeal and sound like they know what they're talking about, I'm more than likely to send them records."

The best way to develop a rapport with publicists is to find the ones who respect zines. There are lots of them out there. Since most zines cover emerging trends and new artists, publicists are usually happy to provide you with access to their breaking artists and product.

> The best way to develop a rapport with publicists is to find the ones who respect zines.

"For the kind of comics we do, it is particularly important to have them reviewed in fanzines," says Chris Jacobs, director of promotions and marketing at Fantagraphics, an underground comics company in Seattle, Washington. "If there are zines I like, I will send them a handful of our stuff. If someone requests comics to review, I'll ask them to send me a copy [of their zine] to see what their editorial direction is. It's more for my own education than anything else. There is pretty much no such thing as bad press."

Still, despite the general love of fanzines amongst fans of counterculture—some of whom hold mainstream jobs that allow them to promote cool stuff—a certain level of professionalism is required. The best way to approach a publicist is to send him or her a package including the best issues of your zine (limit it to three), a note explaining what your interests are, and a statement saying something about how often you plan to publish (if you know).

Then follow up with a phone call. Be patient while waiting for a return call. If what you're covering is out of the mainstream, chances are the office working it is understaffed and will get back to you as soon as they have time. On the other hand, if you send them something, call them once a week for two consecutive weeks, and they *still* don't acknowledge your existence, don't waste your time—or try again after you're more established.

"I don't have an assistant," says Kathy Koehler, publicist for Epitaph Records, "so I rely a lot on voice mail, and what I hate is when people call and go 'Hi, this is John. I want to talk to Rancid. Call me back.' I don't know where they're from and what they do. I like it when someone sends me a zine and a little note. Either I'll call them or they can follow up. Be somewhat professional about it. I have to be professional with the bands so I do need information from zines. But I have more fun talking to the zine kids than magazines. They're not as into the critical thing and they're there 'cause they love loud music and it's a new experience for them. It does disillusion me when kids are just scamming, but I can usually figure that out. That makes me mad because there are so many hardworking zine kids out there."

Whether you have several issues out or not, don't call a business and ask to be added to their overall mailing list. You'll appear greedy and be far less likely to receive the mailings you really want. It's a better idea to call and request individual items. Eventually a publicist will add you to the mailing lists he or she thinks fit your zine. At Epitaph Records, for example, they have a detailed database which is constantly being updated to make sure the proper people receive certain items.

"Our database is structured to keep track of who is publishing and who writes about our stuff and likes it," says Koehler. "We have a lot of fanzines in our database. We track [them] each time we get an issue and file it. Who we mail to is based on who we correspond with. We might enter a fanzine in our database from *Factsheet Five,* but sometimes the correspondence part doesn't happen. Circulation comes into play. There is the case where the kid is putting out 50 copies just so they can get free stuff from the companies—but more often than not they really want to do it. I think we try and base it more on their interest in our kind of bands, and if they care. If it's just a photocopy and small, I still think it's worthy. I do try and support fanzines that are new. It's just hard. You don't want to be taken for a ride."

WHEN THE TABLES TURN

When you reach the point of having publicists call *you* for reviews or interviews, be nice. It's their job to promote the people they represent. The good ones will be familiar with your zine and not bother you with irrelevant information. If they do pitch stories that are of no interest to you, simply tell them, politely, that you don't think that person or topic fits your zine, and reiterate what you cover.

THE IMPORTANCE OF CIRCULATION

Whether or not the circulation of your zine makes any difference to the publicist depends on the individual and the type of business you're contacting. As Kathy Koehler noted, circulation does make a difference, even to some indie businesses. Publicists might not want it to, and they definitely do make exceptions, but, generally speaking, the larger and wider your circulation, the better your access.

Exactly what an adequate circulation is and how much difference it makes varies drastically depending on the publicist and the artist or personality. It tends to make the most difference when you are dealing with a large, corporate entity. Even if you find a zine-friendly publicist, he or she may be restricted by corporate policy. For example, the first ten advance demo tapes of a major artist will go out to the largest national magazines. Don't be jealous. They receive the first advances, but they don't have anything like the freedom of a fanzine. You'll probably receive the advance eventually. "I like to include zines on my list," says Wendy Weisberg, "but sometimes we have [a] more select mailing for the initial 50 advance cassettes. Then in a month or two we'll send to our next tier of people. When [an artist] gets higher-profile management, they want to see the national stuff placed even when it's a new artist."

On the other hand, many publicists believe that, even though the circulation of a zine may be smaller, the likelihood of selling a record to each person who reads the review in a fanzine is higher, because zine readers tend to be passionate about their subject.

"Bands realize that there may only be 500 copies of a fanzine, but the kids who read it are really interested in what the zines have to say," says Koehler. "They're not passive readers. Someone can pick up a copy of *Spin* or *Rolling Stone* and glance through it but not go, 'I have to have that record.' One kid gives a copy of a zine to five of his friends. The fanzine stuff really seems to work. It's great word of mouth."

With other publicists, like independent Jenny Bendel, owner of Plain Jane Publicity, circulation makes almost no difference. Bendel has helped promote the careers of The Presidents of the United States of America, The Jim Rose Sideshow Circus, Supergrass, and Ice T. Bendel's expertise is launching bands from scratch, which she does with the help of a strong network of fanzines.

> Don't think it needs to come out and be glossy right away.

"Circulation doesn't really matter," says Bendel. "I'm looking more for the effort that is going into it. Fanzines are free and they get dropped off in record stores and clubs and that is where the people that are going to buy these records go. If they only drop 50 copies off, that means that 50 people are going to pick it up and read about my band. Even if it's not well-written and if they sound like a 12-year-old who listened to the record and wrote what they felt, that's OK. It doesn't matter if it has a color cover or is just copied and stapled together. They're all great.

"Start slow; start small," Bendel continues. "Don't think it needs to come out and be glossy right away. Cover what you like and don't be pressured by people like me to put in things you don't like. Anyone that's interested in doing any kind of alternative media I think is wonderful."

THE NUTS AND BOLTS OF INTERVIEWING

Back to that Jack LaLanne interview, or any interview for that matter. Generally, a publicist will assist you to the best of his or her ability; nevertheless, getting an interview often depends more on the person you want to talk to than on the publicist. Keep in mind:

- Some individuals simply dislike interviews.
- Others only want to do interviews with specific publications or people.

- When an individual reaches a certain level of awareness in the public consciousness, he or she simply does not have the time to meet all interview requests. On the other hand, that doesn't mean your zine might not be one of the chosen few.

"The majority of our bands are very good about doing fanzine interviews," says Kathy Koehler. "Some of them, that is all they'll do. Rancid is one of our biggest bands and I still set up zine interviews for them. It's just a little harder to coordinate. Every one of our bands have hit the fanzine level before they hit the national press level."

Once again, with a more corporate entity, although the rules are different, it's not a problem. After all, most fanzines exist to provide information not accessible through the mainstream media. Remember that working with publicists is a cooperative effort. Respect their time and responsibilities. All publicists have a job, which is to promote their clients; therefore most publicists prefer to be familiar with the people who they set up interviews with. The way a publicist becomes familiar with your work is by reading your fanzine and having repeated phone conversations with you. A publicist also needs to make sure the person he or she represents uses the interview time effectively. If the publicist sets up a slew of interviews with fanzines and none of them get printed, the publicist may lose his or her job.

"If I already have a relationship with the zine, it's no problem to get an interview, depending on the band's time," says Jenny Bendel. "I don't treat the zine interviews any differently than anyone else. I know some zines feel jilted and wonder how come they're only getting 20 minutes on the phone with someone. Well, the [daily paper] only gets 20 minutes on the phone with them as well. I try to treat them as equally as possible because nine times out of ten they're the people who are going to support my band."

HOW TO BREAK
THE 20-MINUTE RULE

The 20-minute rule tends to be a standard. Press days are set up for an interviewee and on these days he or she spends one 20-minute block of time after another talking to writers. Luckily, many artists ignore these restrictions. This is how the 20-minute rule bends—and it can be both in your favor and against it:

- When you interview someone, try to find a topic which interests him or her. Then he or she will jabber on far longer than 20 minutes. It's your job to make the interview interesting and, in a sense, steal someone else's time.

- If the person who interviewed your person right before you called was particularly interesting, you may get a call late, or not at all.
- Rescheduled interviews are not unusual, and neither is receiving a call up to two hours after an agreed time. Always be prepared to reschedule interviews with people who are busy, chatty, or flaky.

AVOIDING PUBLICISTS

Yes, there are ways to avoid all the rigmarole with publicists. You can either write about your own community, track people down via mail or e-mail, or approach a national figure after a performance.

All these methods are much more casual and less competitive than dealing with publicists. They're also more fun.

Consider starting with your local community. It's always best to start with the folks that surround you, regardless of topic. Not only will you share a common culture because of your geographic location, but also chances are you will both be starting out in your respective projects. To approach local people, ask someone for an introduction; write them a letter; approach them in a public setting. Just step up after a show, reading, lecture, whatever, tell them you respect their work, let them know what your zine covers, and ask for an interview, either on the spot or in the future (their choice). If you want to go this route, then of course it's essential to carry a tape recorder with fresh batteries and an extra tape.

This method also works with better-known folk. You may get rejected, but you should get used to your face hitting the pavement. It happens to everyone, a lot. Generally, the more well-known a person is, the less likely they are to talk to you. They may be tired of talking to folks about their activities, and prefer to let their work speak for itself. Some may think you're an annoying twerp; others may take pity on you—or they might just think your idea is the coolest thing to hit the planet. You never can tell. Chances are you have hip friends doing the things you want to cover. Talk to them. Local people want the publicity, and they're starting out at the same place you are.

MAIL AND ON-LINE INTERVIEWS

Other increasingly common ways to conduct interviews for fanzines are through the mail or on-line. These are less spontaneous than live interviews, but have their benefits as well. Send someone a list of questions, they respond—simple. You get to ask about what you really want to know, and the timing gives the subject a chance to mull over his or her answers, which gives you more thoughtful, if less spontaneous, interplay. Finding the address, however, is up to you. Lots of times people list contact addresses on their work, although mail sent there may be handled by someone else, so you'll be taking your chances whether it actually reaches your person or not.

> ...It's only ethical to let someone know they're participating in an actual interview.

E-mail addresses also are an excellent way to get an interview, provided you're sure the actual person is at the other end. Talking by e-mail can either be like a mail interview, where the person responds at a later time, or done live, which results in a chattier tone. And remember that, as in *all* cases with on-line interviewing, it's only ethical to let someone know they're participating in an actual interview.

STORIES SANS INTERVIEWS

If someone refuses to chat with you, keep in mind that just because you don't get an interview doesn't mean *you* can't spout. Oftentimes, your own opinions about someone's work and life can be far more intriguing than an interview with a person who is uncommunicative. Not everyone wants to be a star. On the other hand, a good many folks who assume the alterna-snob purist posture really love publicity. Still others are just plain moody, and you have to catch them at the right minute and hope you don't inadvertently pluck the emotional string which clams them up. Doing an essay on a topic or person gives your opinion of them, which, unless you use a Q&A interview format, is essentially what you're doing anyway. A good essay without an interview is always better than a Q&A piece where the person refuses—or is simply unable—to communicate in an interesting manner.

CONDUCTING AN INTERVIEW

There are three basic qualities that make for a good interview:

- Experience, which comes with practice;
- Preparation, which requires research;
- Chemistry, for which you need luck.

There are also some basics when it comes to conducting an interview:

- Be yourself, but be polite.
- If you're interviewing a smart-ass and you can respond in kind, do it.
- Don't bluff about what you don't know. People can tell—which brings us to preparation:
- Before you interview someone, know their body of work.
- Know their history—bone up by reading everything you can about them or their area of expertise.

During the interview, go ahead and verify the historical information you have read. Not only is the world packed with mediocre journalists, but miscommunication is simply rampant, and people, especially those involved with countercultures, lie—and they can enjoy pulling a writer's leg. Don't buy into it. The amount of erroneous information floating around is flabbergasting.

It's also important to double-check your interpretation of what the person said to you. You do this by paraphrasing someone's statement back to them. For example:

Subject: I spent my early years in San Francisco.
Zine: So you spent your childhood in San Francisco?
Subject: No, I was going to U.C. Berkeley, that's when I started channeling spirits.

Some people are hard to interview, others won't shut up, or talk incessantly about a topic not relevant to you or the conversation, but obviously very interesting to them for some odd reason. Handle the first type, the quiet one, by asking open-ended questions; questions that can't be answered with a yes, no, or one-word answer.

Not, "Do you like New York?"

"Yes."

Or: "How is New York?"

"Hot."

But, "How has New York affected your work?"—which will at least garner the response, "It helps," at which point you get to ask why.

Starting out questions with the phrase "What do you think," is also dangerous, because a defensive respondent will simply turn it around and ask you what you think instead, although they will occasionally build on your response.

Getting and conducting a successful interview can prove a challenge. It also proves enlightening. Nothing can deflate admiration like discovering a brilliant artist or thinker is a jerk. But that's all part of the fun. What other reason is there to put out a zine except to learn? One of the first skills you must master, however, is the tricky balance between being persistent and polite. Once you develop that skill, in most cases, access will not be a problem.

GRUMPY OLD EDITORS

Fanzines are a free forum for expression, but someone still has to organize the copy, not to mention make sure everything makes sense. In addition to providing hints on editing and developing a positive relationship with your writers (if you have them), this chapter explores the various ways to approach a story. Hopefully you and your contributors already know how to write freely. Obeying rules and someone's else structure can prove the death of creativity; it's always fun to see something different. Don't let traditional forms limit you—they're boring. People see them every day in mainstream papers and look to writers in fanzines as innovators. The best way to explore form is by reading—poetry, literary journals, other zines, children's books, anything. What follow are merely guideposts in case you lose your way. In this chapter you'll learn how the various forms of story structure work, how to deal with writers, and how to edit for space, structure, and grammar.

STORY STRUCTURE

Once you have the information, it's time to figure out a good way to present it—what story form to take. The best idea or interview can be turned into something incomprehensible if it's not properly presented. These five forms are the staples of most writing:

- Reverse pyramid;
- Information bites;
- Essay;
- Q&A;
- Stream of consciousness.

REVERSE PYRAMID

This is the traditional form of news stories. It's a tad trite, but still useful for getting info out succinctly. The reverse-pyramid style starts with a traditional news lead and then addresses information in order of *descending* importance.

The Lead

A lead is the first line or paragraph of a story. It sets the piece up by introducing readers to the topic. It also helps them decide whether or not to continue reading the article so it needs to grab their attention. A traditional news lead answers six questions: who, what, when, where, why, and how.

> *Example:* CoCA (Center for Contemporary Art) [who], in Seattle, Wash. [where] held a three-day conference on fanzines [what], January 12–14 [when]. The event drew underground publishers from across the nation [how] to discuss both the practical and philosophical aspects of publishing a zine [why].

Now that you know what a lead is *supposed* to include, ignore it. Ask a question; paint a picture with words; do *something* to nab the reader's attention while letting them know what the story is about.

Additional Paragraphs

Additional paragraphs expound on the lead. They tell you who was there, what was done, and why it was done. Continuing with the CoCA example:

> *Backup Paragraphs Example:* Keynote speaker, Thomas Frank, editor-in-chief of the *Baffler* in Chicago, launched the workshops, which started on Saturday, by addressing the CultureTrust™ and the co-opting of counterculture by the mainstream. The actual conference started on Friday with musical performances by Miss Murgatroid, Vaginal Creme Davis, and Sleater-Kinney.
>
> Panels examined a variety of topics including the basics of publishing, the danger of censorship and importance of First Amendment Rights, the Internet, and the future of self-publishing. The convention also hosted an exposition where independent publishers sold their wares, including self-published books, fanzines, comics, and papers.

Naturally, a reverse-pyramid style can include quotes and continue endlessly, but it's a little dry. If you're writing something longer but want to be succinct, try to engage the reader with a mutated form of the traditional style: present the most interesting information in the first three or four paragraphs. It makes the person want to read the story. For yourself, just answer the question: Why is this person, event, or thing important? Also, go ahead and include some of the information you assume readers already know, in case some-one's kid brother picks up the zine and becomes enlightened by accident. It *will* happen.

INFORMATION BITES

Thank *USA Today* for popularizing this gem. Information bites are a less formal and more popular way of conveying the same type of information disseminated in a reverse-pyramid style. When you use information bites, you assume readers already know something about the topic or don't care about its history. In addition to taking less space, information presented like this is simpler to read and less stodgy and pretentious than the reverse-pyramid form. You could say the style was developed for people with short attention spans. Here is the same CoCA example as an information bite:

> When you use information bites, you assume readers already know something about the topic or don't care about its history.

CoCA [who] held its first annual symposium on self-publishing [what] Jan. 12 to 14 [when] in Seattle [where]. In addition to an array of panels ranging from how to start your own zine to censorship and publishing on the Internet, the event featured performances by an variety of underground musicians from the West Coast, including Miss Murgatroid, Vaginal Creme Davis, and Sleater-Kinney. Keynote speaker Thomas Frank, editor-in-chief of the *Baffler* in Chicago, launched the workshops, which started on Saturday, by addressing the CultureTrust™ and the co-opting of counterculture by the mainstream.

You'll note that the "why" and "how" questions are not answered. That's the primary problem. This style tells people what went on, but fails to explain why it's relevant.

Essay

This is the classic form in which to give an opinion, so it's well suit-
ed for zines. You can argue an idea or philosophy, present a concept,
or comment on popular culture. It works as follows:

- Pick a topic.
- Make a list of supporting points.
- Arrange them in a logical manner.
- Draw a conclusion.

Yes, at first, it is as hard as it sounds. With practice, many people—
at least those who took debate in high school—skip the outline stage
and simply rant. Remember to back up your main points and not
stray into areas which fail to support your thesis. Of course, if you've
got a touch for doing it well, straying can actually add to the essay,
but that's for you to experiment with.

Example Thesis Outline:
- Thesis: Fanzines are fun to do, but require work and a significant
  financial outlay.
- Point One: Fanzines allow you to state your opinion and obsess
  freely about your favorite topic.
- Point Two: If you want people to read your fanzine, the topic
  should be interesting and the writing must be legible and intelli-
  gible. Although there may only be a small audience that shares
  your obsession, that's okay, because financial gains and large distribution are not the reasons one puts out a zine.
- Point Three: There are lots of ways to produce a fanzine, including cut-and-paste and copying, computer layout and copying,
  computer layout and printing, and full-on color production done
  either by computer or in the traditional pasteup methods, both of
  which require professional printing.
- Point Four: If you choose to publish a fanzine on computer, purchasing both the software and hardware can be expensive. Think
  about whether you can scam computer-time at work or borrow
  a friend's computer until you get serious about putting out a
  high-quality zine.
- Point Five: Some printers are shady, or perhaps it's just that they
  lack communication skills. Not only must you shop around for
  the best deal, but you have to keep on it to make sure your sales
  rep keeps his or her end of the bargain. If you are reproducing

fewer than 1,000 issues, a neighborhood copy shop is always a good alternative.

- Conclusion: Fanzines are fun, but since they are expensive to produce and obsessions change quickly, it's best to start small and learn as you go.

Q&A

This method, along with the stream-of-consciousness style, is one of the basics of the zine world. Like the music zine *maximumrocknroll,* many people feel a complete, unedited Q&A is the only honest way to present an interview; however, others disagree and view unedited interviews as droning pieces of adulation. Artists' viewpoints on this also vary. If you do a mail interview, it would probably be nice to keep things intact. On the other hand, most folks don't mind if someone cleans out the "ums," "ands," and "ers" from a tape-recorded conversation. You might also have to edit an interview down so it fits the space on the page—if so, do it carefully and don't change the meaning of what someone says.

There are lots of ways you can present a Q&A story. An introduction works well. It can do any of the following:

- Tell the reader why the person interviewed is significant.
- Update the audience on the accomplishments of the subject.
- Provide a historical portrait of the person.
- Paint a picture of the setting in which the interview took place to give the reader a feel for the environment.

Regardless of how hip a subject's reputation may be, a boring interview will result in a lackluster Q&A piece. In those instances, it's probably best to convert the interview into a story form. In that case, it's important to keep what a person says in context. Sure you can let them hang themselves with their own words, but it's unethical to force a person's comments into a context where you're making him or her say something other than what was intended. Otherwise you, as editor, come across like a media strategist in a political campaign. It's a fine line to walk, but your gut will let you know. If you feel uneasy about your interpretation, you are probably taking something out of context.

STREAM OF CONSCIOUSNESS

How does one define stream of consciousness? Well, when you write something which sounds like the conversation you have with your brain as you stroll around the lake, that's your consciousness streaming out onto the page.

BEING AN EDITOR

As editor and publisher, you're responsible for everything that appears in your zine. If the design and cover are sloppy or if the content is swamped with spelling errors, you, personally, look inept. More importantly, if you print a piece that is untrue, the person in the story can sue the publication if he or she can prove the story caused him or her harm. If you publish a story about bad landlord experiences and the piece contains inaccurate information about a particular building, the owner can sue you. (Libel is further explained in the next chapter.) As editor, it is your responsibility to fact-check the information in your zine. If a writer pens a piece which incriminates someone, it is best to verify the story. People lie, and if you print those lies, you're liable. Opinions are great, half-truths are reprehensible. On the other hand, satire is art and protected by the First Amendment—but even there you can get in trouble. Yes, the First Amendment is under attack and you too have the right to test it, but that process could prove expensive.

> If a writer pens a piece which incriminates someone, it is best to verify the story.

Another difficult aspect of editing is working with writers. Unless everyone who contributes to your zine is great, you will have to edit for spelling, grammar, and maybe content.

Content editing is touchy because, historically, zines allow people to speak their piece, regardless of how poorly or wildly they say it. How you strike the balance between coherence and freedom for your writers is up to you. Usually the best thing is just to talk to a person about what you want to change and to come to some sort of mutual agreement on the wording. The final decision is yours. Still, respect dictates that, if the person prefers you remove his or her name from the piece after a drastic rewrite, you should honor the request. The other options are to be a tyrant and simply disregard the feelings of your writers—although you will soon find yourself sans writers—or to be completely hands-off, which, unless you have a magical staff, will result in a poor quality zine. You can, of course, also write your entire zine yourself, which isn't a bad idea and eliminates the headache of dealing with writers altogether.

EDITING

There are three main things for which one edits:

- Space.
- Structure.
- Grammar, style, and spelling (copyediting).

Editing for structure is difficult, while correcting grammar is deceptively easy. Unfortunately, editing for space often means cutting something down, which can be just plain torturous, especially if the story is good. After those three steps and the layout process are completed, a proofreader checks everything for the final time. A well stocked reference shelf makes editing much easier. It should include:

- *The Associated Press Stylebook and Libel Manual*. It's the standard stylebook for the publishing industry which is used by all daily newspapers and most magazines. Yes, it's corporate, but the *AP Stylebook* provides answers to most linguistic oddities and will come in handy when you can't find the answer anyplace else.
- A good dictionary, like *Merriam Webster's Collegiate Dictionary.*
- A thick thesaurus.
- A grammar book (my favorite is the *Little, Brown Handbook* though some favor *The Chicago Manual of Style*). These books answer questions that are always popping up, like when to use italics, or does one spell out or use a numeral for 100,000 at the beginning of a sentence? (The answer is to spell it out.) They also make for good reading for people obsessed with language. Really.

EDITING FOR SPACE

Editing for space simply means shortening a story that is too long for the room available—whether that's a page or the general size of the zine. If you can, it's always best to let the writer cut the story. With the more flexible deadlines of zine publishing, there is really no reason not to let the writer do it. Cutting for length should be done *before* the item is proofed and preferably before it is copyedited.

EDITING FOR STRUCTURE AND CONTENT

In zines, you don't *have* to edit for structure or content. In fact, it's unusual to do so. On the other hand, some people want their zine to be of a certain quality. To achieve this quality, they edit and work with their writers or won't print writers who lack talent. There are two interlocking points to keep in mind:

- People don't have to know how to write to have good ideas or philosophies.
- Good ideas and philosophies have to be well presented in order for readers to understand them.

Originality and presentation are obviously less essential if your zine contains Q&A pieces on comic artists than if it features an essay questioning, say, the paramilitary aspects of the Girl Scouts. The best way to edit the latter type of story is to ask the writer about a point that is unclear, or debate the logic of the story with the person who wrote it. It helps to indicate how the piece fails to communicate a specific point, or where the idea gets lost or confused because of poor structure.

Always be respectful of your writer's feelings. A writer may believe an editor is discounting his or her ideas when he or she is asked to rewrite something. But as an editor, it's important that you avoid changing the point a writer is trying to make. If you find his or her ideas upset you to the point where you want to change them, ask yourself whether the ideas are in tune with the vision of your zine. Perhaps that particular writer should not contribute to your zine at all. Zines are meant to be a free expression of ideas for both the editor *and* the writer.

EDITING FOR GRAMMAR AND SPELLING

Editing for grammar is much less painful, but even more necessary. Why? If your zine is full of grammatical and spelling errors, people will question your basic intelligence. Who wants to read this kind of material? One might consider spelling and punctuation secondary to ideas, but ideas cannot be effectively communicated without proper grammar. It exists for a reason—to help communicate thoughts clearly and concisely.

Of course, you can break these rules for effect, but in doing so, make sure your ideas remain clear. Test your style by having someone else read the material. You can use the same system to clarify the

importance of grammar to a writer. Ask him or her what is meant by the sentence that's puzzling you and explain why it is not clear. For example:

Genine ran home with her Dalmatian, panting all the way.

Who was panting? Genine or the dog? Ask this question and the writer will—let's hope—see the need for a rewrite. If there is time, ask the writer to rework the article, so he or she retains ownership and doesn't feel like the editor is destroying the story. You might come up with, *Genine ran home with her Dalmatian, and they were both panting all the way,* while the writer would prefer, *Genine ran home with her Dalmatian. The dog was panting all the way.*

In addition to editing for clarity, you also have to look at the simpler aspect of basic grammar and consistency in style. Below you'll find a list of common grammar and wording errors. Watch for them in both the copyediting and proofing process:

Age: When an adjective precedes a noun, use hyphens: *A 12-year-old boy.* When the description follows the noun, forgo hyphens: *The boy is 12 years old.*

A, an: Use *a* when a word starts with a consonant or a letter you can hear. Use *an* for words starting with a vowel or soft consonant: *an hour* or *an ache,* but *a heart* or *a universe.*

Accept/except: You *accept* (take/receive) an award, but you like all vegetables *except* (excluding) bean sprouts.

A.D./B.C. stands for *anno Domini* (in the year of the Lord) and *before Christ.* Use periods.

Affect/effect: *Affect* is usually a verb and *effect* is the result of a verb. For instance: He said, "These drugs don't *affect* my playing at all"—but you could tell they severely *affected* his sense of rhythm. Then his bandmates put the no-drugs rule into *effect,* and the *effect* of the change was noticeable.

Ain't: Ignore your mother, go ahead and use it.

All ready/already: *All ready* means ready to go, *already* means that something has *already* happened.

A lot is two words.

All right is two words, although it is frequently misspelled in record titles like *The Kids Are Alright* and the contraction will probably become an eventual alternate spelling.

A.m./p.m.: Use lowercase letters with periods.

Book titles: Use italics for these: *The Autobiography of Malcolm X.*

Brackets: Are used to show the editor made a change in what someone said or wrote. They can also go in place of a word or phrase which is quoted when the item needs clarification. "I went to the store and bought the new Nirvana record," he said, versus, "I went to the store and bought *[In Utero]*," he said.

D.C. as in District of Columbia; Washington, D.C. Use periods.

Disc as in compact disc. **Disk** as in computer disk. Hard disk. Floppy disk.

E.g.: Lowercase, periods with no space, followed by a comma. Means "for example." Same for **i.e.,** which means "that is."

Et al. Means "and others": Al, Bett, Courtney, *et al.* (that is, the whole crowd).

Group nouns: Trio, band, quartet are nouns that are singular, so their verbs need to match: "The band *is* going on tour."

Hyphens: *The AP Stylebook* defines them best: "Use them to avoid ambiguity or to form a single idea from two or more words:" She had *purplish-red* hair (not purplish, red hair) and produced her zine by the *cut-and-paste* method.

Improvisator: Watch the spelling—"or," not "er."

It's is a contraction of "it is." *It's* going to fall in an earthquake.

Its is the possessive for the article "it." I like her lake; *its* water is warm.

L.A. stands for Los Angeles. Use periods.

Lay (lay, laid, laid), lie (lie, lay, lain): "Lay" is something someone does to something else. I went to *lay* the zine on the nightstand. It's the same place I have always *laid* my zines. I *laid* it there last night. "Lie" is something someone does. I *lay* in bed all day, just as I have *lain* in bed every Sunday morning this month. The cats like to *lie* there too.

Lineup is one word.

Lose/loose: You *lose* your computer disk, but you like to wear your clothing *loose*. Remember that "loose" has something extra.

Media is plural. You get news through the *media* but communicate through a *medium*.

Magazine and fanzine names are italicized: *Factsheet Five*.

MC means Master of Ceremonies, currently used by hip-hop artists, such as MC Hammer.

Monetary amounts: Do not use decimals for round figures. $10 (not $10.00), but $10.50.

Movie titles are italicized. *The Piano.*

Newspaper titles: Italicized. *The Village Voice*—but watch for the *New York Times.*

Numbers: Spell out one to nine, use numerals for 10 or more. Numbers at the beginning of a sentence are spelled out.

OK, according to the *AP Stylebook*. Spelling it out as "okay" is a common but less preferred variation.

Over/more than: Over is a spatial concept. For example: He hovered *over* (as in above) the crowd. But, "They sold *over* a million books" is incorrect. It should be, "They sold *more than* a million books."

PA as in Public Address System. No periods, no space.

Percent: Use the word instead of the symbol: "*40 percent.*"

Principal/principle: A *principal* leads something or is the overriding factor in something. Her *principal* reason for leaving was the narrow-minded views expressed by her boss. A *principle* is something one lives by. Her boss had no *principles.*

Sit/set: This is very similar to lay and lie. *Set* (set, set, set) means to set *something* somewhere. *Sit* (sit, sat, sat) is an *action*. You *set* your butt on the sofa but you *sit* on the sofa.

Subject/verb agreement: Although a phrase such as "I is ugly" will jump out for you to fix, you might have to look harder for inaccuracies such as "The trio are jamming." (Trio is a singular noun.)

Rock 'n' roll has two apostrophes around the 'n.' The apostrophes stand for the letters that have been taken away from either side.

Than/then: *Than* is a preposition usually used for comparison, and *then* communicates time: "I like coffee better *than* herbal tea. I drank some herbal tea, and *then* followed it with coffee."

Their/there/they're: *Their* is a possessive adjective, *there* defines place, and *they're* is a contraction of "they are." For example: *Their* van was stolen. I love New York and I want to move *there*. *They're* unhappy you chose to convey that opinion.

Titles: Italicize titles of albums, EPs, CDs, books, movies, magazines, newspapers, TV series, artworks, and ships. Titles of articles in magazines, songs and singles, stories, radio shows, and single television programs go in quotation marks, for example, "Smells Like Teen Spirit." Note that prepositions *(at, by, for, from)*, conjunctions *(and, but, or)* and articles *(the, an, a)* of three characters or fewer are not capitalized in titles, unless, of course, they are the first or last word in the title.

T-shirt: Capital T, followed by a hyphen.

Which/who: Use *which* for inanimate objects and *who* for people (and, in my opinion, animals—anything that has a gender).

Years: *'93, '80s, 1990s.* Put an apostrophe at the beginning of a year that does not start with the millennium, for example, *'93.* To start a sentence use *Nineties.* (I assume, however, that we will start using full years for 2002, at the start of the next millennium, at least for the first decade.) Do not put an apostrophe between the last number and the *s* (like 1960s) unless it is a possessive.

> *Most good writers don't mind spending a day perusing a grammar book, dictionary, or thesaurus.*

If you are unfamiliar with any grammatical term referenced in this chapter, pick up a style book and research it. If you plan to put out a fanzine, you inevitably read and probably know the concepts but not the terms that describe them. Most good writers don't mind spending a day perusing a grammar book, dictionary, or thesaurus. There's always something to learn. If it scares you, break down and take a formal class, but do not let the instructor destroy your style. As a writer you need to have your own voice, not a generic one! The same holds true for a college or high-school paper. If it's too stodgy, start your own. Once again, make sure it's grammatically correct (unless you're deliberately breaking the rules for style, of course); otherwise, your writing can lose its edge.

THE FINAL COPYEDIT, AND EDITING FOR STYLE

After you read copy for content and grammar, review it again and search for the mistakes previously listed, as well as proper punctuation (periods, commas, semicolons, parentheses, etc.), spelling (including names and locations), dates, and style.

STYLE SHEETS

"Style" refers to rules listed on a style sheet. All major publications create them to guarantee that certain items are handled consistently throughout the book. For instance, should "OK" appear as *O.K., OK,* or *okay?* If it doesn't matter, you don't need a style sheet. If such inconsistencies bother you, start jotting them down now. The list will inevitably grow. Style sheets include instructions on:

- How to designate time, and how to handle numbers.
- How words with various spellings will be handled, and which words get hyphens.
- How items will be spelled and capitalized, including people's names, and special terms.
- How to abbreviate state names.
- Where capitalization should be used in headlines and subheads.
- Anything else you want presented with consistency.

Style sheets add polish to a zine, but they aren't necessary for a casual project. If you're putting out a zine on your own, the style sheet will most likely be stored in the recesses of your brain. As a rule, writers tend to either gripe about or ignore style sheets since they sometimes feel these documents infringe upon their individual expression. Like grammar, style should be flexible.

PROOFREADING

Proofreading is the final step in the editing process. It takes place after the copy has been "set"—handwritten, typed, word processed, whatever—but before it goes to the printer. Proofreaders go over the copy one last time and look for the mistakes everyone else has missed. They:

- Check the spelling of names and titles.
- Verify dates.
- Look for the grammar errors previously noted in this chapter.
- Make sure that a story flows properly (no copy is missing or repeated).
- Check for correct *page jumps.* Page jumps are a frequent place for mistakes to happen. If a story is continued on a page that does not immediately follow the previous page, it's nice to have a "jump" indicating on which page the story continues; e.g., *continued on page 15,* and, on page 15, *continued from page 10.*
- Make sure the name of the person writing the story is correct!
- Check for orphans and widows—single lines separated from a paragraph at the bottom or top of a column. You can ignore widows and orphans if you want. They're a wonderfully time-consuming obsession for perfectionists.

A couple of hints for successful proofing:

- Even if you do everything else in your zine—write it, edit it, lay it out—you should have someone else proof it. It prevents embarrassing mistakes.

- It's also best to have someone other than the person who did the copyediting perform the proofreading task. Once the same person has read a piece three or four times, his or her eyes tend to slide over mistakes. Plus, the voice in the back of your brain keeps chanting, "You've read this before; it's error-free," which of course, is rarely true.

FINDING WRITERS AND PRINTING LETTERS

Most zines are written by the one or two people who start them. There are, of course, exceptions. Generally, it is best to recruit your friends, because they probably share whatever interest you have. If your zine grows in size and popularity, people may simply send you items and request that you print them. You can choose to do so or not. In either case, it's nice to write them back. People who read zines tend to be avid correspondents. In fact, starting a zine is an excellent way to make contact with people who share whatever bizarre interest you choose to write about. Most zines do not have a specific area for letters; however, this doesn't mean you can't print them. But if the letter is not clearly marked for publication, use discretion before printing it. It's best to contact the sender both to ask permission and to make sure the letter is not a joke. People do send letters using someone else's name on occasion.

If you find you need writers and your pool of friends does not produce an adequate supply, ask around. Someone who is both handy with a pen and knowledgeable on a particular topic is usually not too hard to find. Getting publicity for your zine is another good way to recruit writers, as Carla DeSantis, publisher of *ROCKRGRL,* discovered after an article on her zine ran in the *Los Angeles Times.*

"I was really lucky because I have had writers donate stuff to me," she says. "The writers understood that there was a need for [a magazine focusing on female musicians]. I couldn't pay them a dime and I still can't." That's OK. Few fanzine contributors ever get paid. It's a labor of love.

Unfortunately, not everyone is as lucky as DeSantis. Jeff Gilbert, publisher of *Mansplat,* receives lots of queries, but finds few people who have the knack of writing copy with the appropriate humor for his zine. Produced on newsprint, the 24-page zine celebrates distinctly male interests such as beer, women, monster movies, and bathroom humor. The zine started with a circulation of 1,000, which grew to 3,000 within a year.

"I write most of *Mansplat,*" says Gilbert. "Then I have Glen and Gregg (two buddies Gilbert has known for more than 20 years) contribute. I've been putting *Mansplat* out for a year and I've had about 30 people contact me, but not very many of them have been in the *Mansplat* frame of mind. They have to be right for the zine. Also, you know how it is, people want to write but when they find out they have deadlines [they flake out]."

> While finding writers is relatively easy, getting rid of them can be emotionally painful both to a publisher and the writer.

While finding writers is relatively easy, getting rid of them can be emotionally painful both to a publisher and the writer. Since writers are essentially freelancers, it's easy to simply say there is not room for their contributions or not to assign them anything for future issues. That is one approach—however, honesty seems to be a better option. Telling someone his or her style or work habits simply don't fit with your vision is probably the quickest and most respectful way to go about it. Make sure to let the writer know that what he or she does or thinks is not wrong, but that it does not fit with what you're doing. You could even suggest that he or she start a zine.

All that dour stuff said, editing is fun. Although not as glamorous as writing, it's yet another way to play with words, and fixing the mistakes of others can sharpen your own word craft. Editing is definitely one of the harder aspects of putting out a zine: It requires a rigorous attention to detail and the grit to ask people to change things; however, strong editing is one of the elements that sets a great zine apart from its sloppy contemporaries.

CHAPTER THREE
LAWS TO IGNORE, OR MAYBE NOT

As far as most fanzines are concerned, laws are like chains—they were made to break—or at least rattle. Still, it's good to know what the laws are as well as the ramifications of breaking them. Aside from copyright, most media laws deal with privacy or libel and are fairly liberal. Of course, there are also pornography laws which, in theory, are supposed to be fairly hard to break. Unfortunately, if you publish racy material, people will give you grief whether you break the laws or not—but you knew that already. The types of print law covered in this chapter include:

- First Amendment;
- Obscenity or pornography;
- Libel;
- Invasion of privacy;
- Copyright laws.

FIRST AMENDMENT RIGHTS

First Amendment rights confuse people. You can *not* print anything you want, and you shouldn't be able to. If you could, then no one could be held responsible for printing lies. What the First Amendment *does* protect may vary depending on what year it is.

Why? Because the First Amendment is subject to interpretation by the Supreme Court and, in a way, all the courts below it. Not every freedom of speech case is heard by the Supreme Court, and you probably couldn't afford to take a court case that far anyway unless you were funded by the American Civil Liberties Union. The good news is that, currently, with the exception of libelous and obscene (whatever that is) material, you can pretty much print anything you want as long as it does not directly advocate the overthrow of the government. A zine can criticize politicians and businesses, advocate illegal acts, and even go as far as saying the government needs to be toppled. What you can *not* do is give specific instructions on where and when to physically topple it. It is important to remember, however, times like the McCarthy era. In the 1950s, a person speaking or writing his or her mind against the government would most likely be investigated and blackballed as a communist. A historical excursion researching the fate of entertainers who criticized the government in the 1950s is essential for anyone concerned with First Amendment rights. Since we're living in another decade, perhaps it's best we address current First Amendment issues, including freedom of expression in schools and prior restraint.

SCHOOLS

Usually you can assume that a student who produces a zine would be held to the same guidelines followed by the students who produce the school paper. If you produce a zine as part of a school project, the institution can limit what you print. The guidelines are broad and vague; a teacher or principal may prevent you from printing just about anything. Considering the manner in which books are banned from school libraries, distributing a zine on campus could prove a royal pain. The easiest solution is to produce and distribute a zine off-campus.

PRIOR RESTRAINT

Prior restraint is a concept most commonly associated with wars. Since you probably won't be covering an international conflict in person, don't worry about the Pentagon limiting your access to

> *If you produce a zine as part of a school project, the institution can limit what you print.*

secret sites (unless they're located in the United States) or reviewing your stories before you copy them at Kinko's. This example does explain the logic behind prior restraint, however. It exists to protect government secrets. In order to prevent you from printing them, a government agency has to prove their exposure would hurt the public good. In all other cases, people cannot prevent you from publishing something because of what you *might* print. A government official, or even your next door neighbor, can't stop you from distributing a zine containing a story about their behavior. That is prior restraint. Likewise, a publisher can't be prosecuted for something they *might* print; however, they can be prosecuted for something they *do* print. If your zine is distributed and contains false information, the person who the false story was about can sue you for libel.

OBSCENITY OR PORNOGRAPHY

This is a charming issue. Since it is based on "community standards" and "artistic value," the law is obtuse and subject to interpretation by judges and juries. The United States has an odd obsession, not to mention a total lack of humor, with regard to sexually explicit material. There is a tendency to blame it for all societal ills, and if you print a risqué zine, someone will inevitably accuse you of causing the downfall of humanity. Good for you. For practical purposes, however, here is how these laws work. In order for a zine to be obscene, it must meet a three-part test:

- The average person in a community (usually defined by a state as the state in which the suit is brought to court) must find the entire zine appeals strictly to the more vulgar aspects of sexuality. In other words, it has to be a perverted sex rag.
- A zine must clearly show or describe lewd sexual behavior as defined by state law.
- The zine must lack literary, artistic, scientific, or political value.

Unless a zine publishes material appealing exclusively to "prurient [lewd] interests," it's difficult to define it as obscene. Unfortunately, that may not stop people from suing, and, consequently, forcing a publisher to spend endless amounts of money on lawyers' fees. There are also other ways that "obscenity" is regulated, primarily by the RICO statutes and the U.S. Postal system. And there are laws involving obscenity and minors.

RICO STATUTES

RICO statutes are another way to control "obscenity." They are similar to "three strike" laws which demand a life sentence after someone is convicted for a third offense. If you break the law by conducting a trade considered corrupt (including the distribution of pornography) three times in a 10-year period, RICO statutes carry up to a 20-year prison term and force the owner of the business to hand over the profits he or she made through the offending business. Basically, this means if someone distributes something the state considers obscene, and he or she is prosecuted three times, the government can seize the business. Unfortunately if you're the owner or publisher, you won't know it is obscene until after you are prosecuted. These statutes probably won't make that much difference to your zine, but they might greatly affect a distributor. In fact, RICO statutes might prevent the distributor from distributing your zine anywhere across state lines.

THE U.S. POST OFFICE

No, you can't send obscene material through the U.S. Postal Service. At one time, it was even illegal to send the racy but classic D.H. Lawrence novel *Lady Chatterley's Lover* through the mail! When a zine is sent through various states to its readers, it can be tried for obscenity in any of the states through which it travels. So if you mail something from Washington to Montana, it can be tried in Idaho. The trick works like this:

- The laws regarding obscenity in your state are lax.
- The Post Office tracks which states your zine travels through via the mail.
- You are tried in the state with the most restrictive laws, even if it is not the zine's final destination.

Cute, huh?

SEXUALITY AND THE UNDERAGE PERSON

Laws that prohibit distribution of "explicit" material to minors are called "variable obscenity laws." There are limitations on these laws. A zine cannot be kept from an underage person simply because it contains nudity. It is, however, illegal to distribute child pornography. Specifically, this means you can't print a photograph of a minor or minors that is sexually explicit.

A RECENT CASE

The most notable case involving a zine and obscenity law took place in Bellingham, Washington, a small college town about a two-hour drive north of Seattle. The town is quiet, liberal, and inhabited by students, artists, university staff, and those employed in businesses which revolve around the university. It seemed an unlikely location for the zine "trial of the century," which involved the owner and manager of a small retail outlet called Newsstand International.

The case centered around a popular annual zine called *Answer*

Me!, produced by Portland, Oregon, resident Jim Goad. It's a satiri-
cal publication which had garnered national attention well before
the lawsuit. Seth Friedman, editor of *Factsheet Five,* voted *Answer
Me!* "the greatest fanzine on the planet." Mainstream journalists also
took note of the publication. *The San Francisco Bay–Guardian* sum-
marized the zine as, "The most elegant document of equal opportunity hatred, outré journalism, and precision rage I've ever seen,"
and *Details* magazine described
Answer Me! #4 as "probably the
hottest fanzine in America."

The problem began when Laura
Bergstrom, a student at Western
Washington University, picked up the
1995 "rape" issue of the zine at
Newsstand International. Upon open-
ing the publication, she unearthed a
narrative by a child molester, a first-
person account of a prison rape, and
an interview with a serial killer. As an
added bonus the zine contained a
fold-out "predator" game board with a
series of prey cards and various rape

> As an added bonus the zine contained a fold-out "predator" game board with a series of prey cards and various rape jokes.

jokes. Bergstrom wrote a letter to the Western Washington University
student newspaper, *The Western Front,* labeling *Answer Me! #4*
pornography, and advocating a boycott of Newsstand International.
The letter got the town talking and resulted in a complaint by the
Whatcom Crisis Center, a service organization which helps abused
women. That complaint prompted an officer of the law to visit
Newsstand International and "suggest" the store stop selling *Answer
Me! #4.* They complied, but did so by swiftly placing the remaining
copies under a chain and padlock, covering the stack with a black
linen cloth, erecting a sign stating the zine was not for sale, and
protesting what they considered censorship. The response received a
lot of publicity which induced Whatcom County Prosecutor David
McEachran to order the fanzines removed, even though they were no
longer available to the public.

"They stopped selling it as soon as the police complained," says
Breean Beggs, attorney for Newsstand International, "but they
couldn't quite lie down without doing something about censorship; **37**

so they put up a little sign. The prosecutor found out, called them to a meeting, and told them he didn't like the zine. He thought it was obscene and they needed to promise never to sell that zine, or anything similar, again. The client said, 'We cannot agree to any of those conditions.'"

On Valentine's Day, 1995, McEachran filed a felony charge against the retailer for promotion of obscenity. If convicted, both the manager and the owner of the store could have faced sentences of up to five years in prison and a $10,000 fine. Fortunately, Newsstand International was found not guilty. "It's mainly a political zine," says Beggs. "Even if it has explicit sex described in it, if it's political, it should be protected [by the First Amendment].

"Unfortunately for fanzine purposes," he continues, "the verdict is somewhat ambiguous. In order to convict Newsstand International, the prosecutor had to prove that the zine was obscene, that my clients sold it intentionally, and that they knew that it was obscene at the time they sold it.

"If the jury found any one of those lacking, it was a not guilty.

"Theoretically, the jury could have found the zine obscene, but that my clients did not know it was obscene. As a practical matter, 11 [jurors] thought the zine wasn't obscene. One person thought it was, but [that Newsstand International] didn't know it. We know what the jury was thinking, but for legal precedent purposes, they didn't sign a questionnaire that said the reason they are not guilty is *this*."

The *Answer Me! #4* saga did not end with the "not guilty" verdict, however. Newsstand International filed a civil suit claiming the Whatcom County Prosecutor had violated its First Amendment rights through prior restraint. It also charged that the initial suit was filed out of retaliation to the display rather than because a law had been allegedly broken. "If someone files a prosecution to shut people up [it violates] their First Amendment rights," says Beggs. "You have a cause of action. You can go to court and argue that it was illegal."

As of press time, the case had yet to go to trial, but Beggs is confident Newsstand International will prevail. He also believes the counter suit will set a precedent for future cases involving fanzines. "Fanzines go back to the way things were when the Bill of Rights was passed," he explains. "[At that time there were all] these self-publishers with all this outrageous political rhetoric. That was what the First Amendment was about. We went through the stage of little presses being shut down and consolidated into big, multimedia giants. Now we are able to go back. As long as people are expressing unpopular opinions, there is going to be this kind of pressure, but the First Amendment says you cannot regulate the content of people's thoughts. Fanzine authors are going to run into this to the degree that they are politically incorrect. This case will be great, once we win it, to show that's protected. It's not illegal to promote illegal things. You can publish a book saying everyone should go out and murder someone. That's not illegal. It is only illegal if you incite a crowd. Fanzines are pushing the limits of people's tolerance. [That's when] you see whether or not the court will uphold the First Amendment."

The initial *Answer Me! #4* case was, to say the least, an intriguing battle and one well worth fighting. A sobering fact, however, is that, according to a report in *The Rocket* magazine, in their countersuit, Newsstand International is asking for an estimated $200,000 in damages to cover legal fees.

LIBEL

Libel is when you print something about someone that damages the person's reputation. Basically, if you print something that is true you are safe. The problem is, people can often accidentally print things that are not true. This can happen when someone you interview gets his or her facts wrong. In libel cases, the type of person being written about makes a difference in the criteria on which the case is judged. The courts divide people into four categories:

- **Public figures:** These are people who are constantly in the media spotlight of a specific community. If your zine is national, this includes entertainers, national politicians, and anyone else who, either purposely or inadvertently, ends up under constant media scrutiny. If your zine covers a small community, this could also include a mayor and well-known local citizens or performers, in addition to national figures.
- **Public officials:** These people can be scrutinized with regard to their actual work or their suitability to do that work. For instance, you can question the fire marshal's regulations as well as his ability to do his job. If he appears drunk at public functions, that is of public interest. If he is having an extramarital affair, it's not.
- **Limited public figures:** These are people who step into the media spotlight in order to effect change in a community. For

example, it could be someone who is highly visible and vocal while working on a political campaign. This would be the type of person who speaks to the media on behalf of an organization. By law, they are treated the same as public officials.

- **Private persons:** Almost complete protection is maintained for persons in private life.

If someone decides to take you to court with a libel suit, the person must prove the following in order to win:

- *That the material was published.* (Well, the plaintiff probably has a copy of your zine, right?)
- *That the material published concerned the plaintiff in the case.* A person can be identified either by photograph, name, or situation, such as "the blonde woman who works the night shift at the 7-Eleven at Fourth and Denny."
- *That the material was published with malice, intent, or negligence.* As a rule, people in the media spotlight must prove that your intent was malicious. In other words, that a printed statement was meant to harm their reputation. A private person must, in most states, merely prove negligence, which means that a zine was too sloppy to double-check its facts before they were printed.
- *That the statements made damaged the person's reputation.* This can include anything from someone's religious beliefs, to political leaning, to sexual behavior.
- *That the statement was false.* However, the degree of this falsity varies, depending on whether the plaintiff is a public or private person. If the plaintiff is a public person—an entertainer, a political figure, or in some other way media-worthy—he or she needs to prove the statement false. If it is a private person, he or she only needs to prove the statement false if it is deemed of public interest.

Examples:
- Someone tells you in an interview that an famous actress has a drug problem. She does not, but you believe the source and print it. If she sued, she would lose the case because she is a public figure and you did not print the information with malice.
- Someone tells you in an interview that the fire marshal has a drug problem. He does not, but you believe the source and print it. If the fire marshal sued, he would probably lose the case because he

is a public official and a drug problem might affect his judgment. However, a judge might very well find you guilty instead, because you were negligent and failed to double-check your facts.

- Someone tells you in an interview that a local activist for the industrial use of hemp has a drug problem. She does not, but you believe the source and print it. In your community, this woman is well known for not smoking, drinking, or using drugs. In fact, she is vegan, eats only vegetables grown without chemicals, and does not drink coffee. She would win the case. Although she is a limited public figure and active in the hemp movement, drug abuse would probably not affect her judgment in a way that hurts society; also, the facts were simple to verify. A judge would find a zine negligent since it failed to double-check information which was easily accessible.

> Libel is the reason why, when mainstream reporters cover someone who is charged with a crime, they use the word "allegedly."

- Someone tells you in an interview that his or her next door neighbor has a drug problem. He does, but it's a well kept secret. If he sued, he would probably win the case because he is a private person, you ruined his reputation, and the information is not of public interest.

Libel is the reason why, when mainstream reporters cover someone who is charged with a crime, they use the word "allegedly." It is a way of saying someone was arrested and charged for an act, but has not been found guilty or innocent at the time the publication went to press. But keep this one important thing in mind: Even if a zine uses the word "allegedly," people may assume the person is guilty. That type of harm is rarely reversible, whether the person is found guilty or not guilty.

INVASION OF PRIVACY

It is rarely libelous to print anything that is true; however, it could be an invasion of privacy. Invasion laws are generally very complicated. They vary from state to state, but can be broken down into three basic areas:

- Intrusion;
- Publication of private information;
- The use of someone's image for commercial purposes.

INTRUSION

Unless you are doing investigative research, it is easy not to break intrusion laws. They are really common sense, and the laws are quite liberal. As long as something happens in a public place, it's fair game. For example:

- It is not intrusion if you take a photograph of someone in a public place. You can take a photograph of someone on the street or even through a window not covered by drapes. You also can photograph people in public businesses, such as restaurants (although the proprietor can throw you out), but not in private clubs—in other words, places that require membership. If you are invited into a private club or home, it is assumed that you may use the information obtained while you are there. Again, it's considered basic good manners to tell a person when he or she is being interviewed.

- In some states it is illegal to record a person with hidden audio or photographic devices. Unless you're doing an investigative piece, recording someone without their knowledge is a bit on the sleazy side anyway. The breakdown is as follows:
  - It is illegal *to record a conversation without the person's knowledge* in California, Delaware, Florida, Illinois, Louisiana, Maryland, Michigan, Oregon, New Hampshire, Pennsylvania, and Washington.
  - It is illegal *to photograph someone with a hidden camera without their consent* in Georgia, Maine, Michigan, New Hampshire, South Dakota, and Utah.

PRIVATE INFORMATION

Since the law is obtuse, it is fairly easy to break laws concerning this aspect of right to privacy. Nevertheless, it is illegal to print information about a person if it is:

- **Highly offensive:** which translates to information which would offend the average person, not the readers of your zine. For instance, you cannot print a photo of a person giving birth without her permission.

- **Not in the public interest:** A story is the public's interest if it informs or enlightens the public on something they need or want to know about. Of course, with highly public people, such as entertainers or politicians, many things are deemed of "public interest" that might not apply to a private person.

What is considered highly offensive or of legitimate public concern depends on a judge or jury. There are, however, certain things that are not considered private. These include:

- Things that happen in public;
- Information of which the majority or at least a large segment of the community is already aware;
- Information in public records.

Examples:

- A local newscaster is arrested for shoplifting. You print his name and make sure to use the word "allegedly" in the charge. He sues you. You would win the case, because police records are public information. Additionally, a newscaster breaking the law is of interest to the public.
- You find "before and after" photos of someone's penile enlargement in the garbage. The photos show his face. You print them. The person sees your zine and sues you. You would lose this case because most people would find this information highly offensive. Additionally, a person's penile enlargement is not in the public interest, nor is it likely something the majority of the public knows about. If you had eliminated the person's face from the photo, printing the images would have been OK because people could not identify him.

THEFT OF IDENTITY FOR COMMERCIAL PURPOSES

You cannot use someone's likeness to sell a product without consent. For example, if you have someone pose in a T-shirt with the name of your zine on it, and you then superimpose the head of a well-known figure onto that image, that well-known figure can sue you if you sell those T-shirts. The photograph implies that the person whose head you used advocates your zine's philosophy and the T-shirts. Be aware that when you use a person's photograph or image, it's important to do so in a way that doesn't imply that they endorse a product. Even when a person poses in something like a T-shirt, you should, in theory, get him or her to sign a release form. It's a little formal for a zine, and whether you choose to do so or not is up to you. A simple release form reads as follows:

> I (name of individual) permit (name of zine) to publish photographs of me. I waive the right to inspect or approve the photograph or copy appearing with the photograph and release (name of zine) from any liability that may result from use of the photograph.

Additionally, people under the age of 18 cannot give consent, and for adults, verbal consent may not stand up in a court of law if a person's life has changed substantially since the time of consent. If you receive verbal agreement to take a pictures of a drag queen in a T-shirt promoting your zine and decide to rerun the photo 15 years later, when the person is a CEO of a conservative corporation, he can sue on the basis that you should have asked him for permission again. Release forms protect you from such situations.

In addition to the aforementioned type of appropriation, there is something known as false light. False light protects an individual from the publication of false information; for example, the use of his or her name in a story involving dramatization, or the use of his or her photograph in a story in which he or she was not directly involved. In order to prove false light, a person must prove that the false information printed was offensive to the average person and that the publisher was at fault; in other words, that the publisher was malicious or knew the facts were not true. There are easy ways to avoid prosecution under this law. If you use dramatization, fictionalize the name of the person and do not print photographs that are not directly involved with a story. For instance, do not use a photo of a generic automobile accident to illustrate the dangers of inattentive drivers. Printing this type of photo implies the driver of the car was at fault and he or she could sue you.

COPYRIGHT LAWS

Zines have a healthy tradition of ignoring copyright laws. Comics are stolen and the text replaced with amusing blurbs, and photos of camp clothing or food are lifted from magazines on a regular basis. For the most part, people who own the original art never even see the mutilations. Yet breaking copyright law can piss people off, so you should at least be aware how the law works, in case someone wants to nail you. Ironically, some zine publishers are now beginning to copyright their own material, so the law can work both ways.

Stealing is not a good way to deal with writer's block!

Copyright protects the way in which a person expresses concepts and ideas—his or her intellectual property. The act of stealing the expression, whether the expression is manifested in art or words, is called *plagiarism*. A fanzine can repeat an idea, concept, or fact, but it cannot do so using someone else's words or images. Stealing is not a good way to deal with writer's block! For fanzines this law works in two ways:

- If you choose to copyright your work, it can prevent someone else from reusing it without permission.
- If you borrow someone else's work—let's say graphics from a '70s ad—they can sue you.

When zines were photocopied and had small distributions, copyright infringement wasn't addressed because nobody took zines seriously. Since many zines now have slick covers and show up on the newsstand at Tower Books, corporations with large legal departments are beginning to send cease-and-desist letters to independent publishers. Such a letter basically tells a zine that if it doesn't stop distributing a particular issue, the corporation will sue.

How to Copyright Material

Traditionally, zines hold copyright laws in disdain, but since people are starting to go for copyright, here's how: Place the word "copyright" and the copyright symbol © next to the date of the publication and the name of the fanzine. For example, if your zine is called *Tadeo,* your copyright notice would look like this: Copyright © 199_ by Tadeo.

This should be protection enough for most zines. If you do ever want to press charges against someone, first you need to register your work. This is also easy. Just write the Library of Congress, Copyright Office, Washington, DC 20559, and send a copy of your zine. They will in turn send you the correct forms. After that simply send them two copies of your zine and a filing fee. Copyright protection conveys to the owner of the material (the person holding the copyright) sole rights to:

- Reproduce the material: For example, you can't legally use a photograph from a magazine without permission.
- Distribute the material: So if you do use that photograph illegally, you are breaking the law again when you distribute it.

FAIR USE

Fair use allows people to reproduce portions of a copyrighted article for the public good. Thus, when one is reviewing a book or other work of art, it is considered "fair use" to quote from that work. It is not, however, fair use to reprint the piece in its entirety. In the end, fair use is primarily determined by whether or not the owner of the copyright can lose money because of what you print. A zine crosses the line of fair use if it prints something the copyright owner plans to market or is selling.

PARODY AND COPYRIGHT

Parody is a large part of many zines. They've always satirized mainstream stuff. Now society, or at least the major corporations who keep it running, are upset. The Mattel company sent a cease-and-desist letter to the publisher of *Hey There Barbie Girl* because it depicted a Barbie Doll wearing only boots gazing into a mirror. The parody was probably quite legal. It made a social comment on the effects Barbie has on our society. She *is* an icon, after all. Unfortunately, Mattel has a lot of money, and the publisher of *Hey There Barbie Girl* didn't. The publisher did not get sued, but she did stop publishing after her second issue. As zines continue to break into the mainstream consciousness, problems like this will increase.

You can use a copyrighted image, as long as *what* you add to it is obviously yours, and the addition or change is obvious; then it is legal to parody it—it's a form of fair use. Basically you have to communicate an opinion or idea about the item you reproduce. Unfortunately, if someone does not like the opinion, they can threaten to sue you. Most major corporations know an independent publisher can't afford to defend his or her work, even if it is legal. One never knows who will react, either. *Bunnyhop* had a cover depicting

Matt Groening's rabbit Binky slugging the Trix rabbit. The makers of Trix either didn't see the cover or didn't care, but the Matt Groening Corporation sent the zine a letter demanding it receive proof of destruction of the remaining copies.

On the whole, if you have respect for people, it's difficult to break laws concerning privacy or libel. Try to poke fun at society or comment on sexuality, however, and people get upset. What's new? This is the reason fanzines exist. As fanzines continue to grow in popularity and as distribution systems designed specifically for zines make them more available to the general public, all these legal issues will eventually encroach on an independent publisher's freedom. If you put out a fanzine that pushes any particular envelope, study the laws which may affect you. It is always important to be aware of the potential consequences your actions may have, whether or not you consider those laws legitimate.

Chapter Four
Advertising and Sponsorships

dvertising in fanzines is a strange thing. So are sponsorships of fanzines. In some sense, zines shouldn't accept either. Supposedly, zines are publications designed for total free expression. They ignore laws and are not affected by outside influences. Unfortunately, it takes money to put out a zine, and if you want to get whatever you're saying out to a large number of people, that cost can be prohibitive. Advertising is definitely the most common method used to help defray costs. Sponsorships are somewhat new and have their own set of benefits and drawbacks. This chapter will examine both the up and the down sides, as well as providing some practical approaches for both these possibilities.

ADVERTISING IN ZINES

If you take advertising, keep in mind:

- You are indebted to your advertisers in only one way: You owe them an ad in the dimension and time frame promised—nothing more.

- Most advertisers who deal with zines are aware that they can't "buy" editorial coverage. In other words, just because someone buys an ad does not mean his or her product gets a good review— or a review at all. Other advertisers will try to exert leverage with their financial power to influence what zines publish. If you let that happen just once, people will know they can do it, and will continue to try to tell you what to print. In the end, it's always better, though it's not always feasible, to publish a zine free of advertising.

- If you decide to take advertising, be selective. You can reject anything you want. Jeff Smith, who publishes *Feminist Baseball,* a pop culture zine covering film, music, literature, and whatever else turns Smith's crank that particular issue, has a great attitude: "That's part of the luxury of having a fanzine," he says. "You can say, 'No this [ad] is stupid. I don't want your $20.' It would be harder to turn down a $10,000 cigarette ad." *(Hint:* most fanzines will never have to worry about R. J. Reynolds calling them.)

IT MIGHT BE EASIER THAN YOU THINK

Once your zine takes off, it might prove surprising just how easy advertising is to come by. Many businesses solicit zines that never even thought of accepting advertising. Why? There are a lot of benefits to advertising in a zine. The advertising is inexpensive—say $20 for the whole back page. Folks who read zines are usually obsessed with the topic the publication covers. For example, someone who reads a fanzine dedicated to vintage clothing probably shops at secondhand stores more than your average daily newspaper reader. Zines also get passed around a lot, which is something advertisers consider. Besides, zines have that elusive quality known as "indie cred," for which the mainstream is always willing to shell out a couple of bucks. Businesses that exist in the counterculture also purchase ads, and zines may reach their customers more effectively than mainstream media. For example, some record companies prefer to advertise in zines.

"For what we are doing it's the only way to go," says Kathy Koehler of Epitaph Records. "Obviously our label caters to a certain genre, and the Punk rock kids live and die by zines. Until recently, that's how people found out about that kind of music. Epitaph started on the basis of fanzines and we do a lot of fanzine advertising."

OPTIONS

Your options are to reject all advertising, take only advertising that you like, or solicit advertising. If you do decide to accept advertising here are some basics to remember:

- Tell whoever is advertising what dimensions you offer. Chances are they will still send you something the wrong size, at which point you will have to call back and ask if they want you to make the ad fit by blowing it up or shrinking it down. You can also put a border around an ad if it is too short or thin. Placing copy between other ads that have borders works well too.

- Inform advertisers of the cost of each dimension. Someone will inevitably send you either a mis-sized ad or the wrong amount of money. At that point, pick up the phone and ask them if they'd rather have you adjust the size or price.

- Tell advertisers approximately how often your zine comes out, how many copies you print, and in which zine their ad will appear.

- When it comes out, send advertisers a copy of the zine that includes their ad.

- Hang up on somebody who calls up and bitches you out because you ran a negative story on something they advertised. OK, you don't have to do that, but you should.

When flipping through zines, you'll note the majority of advertising comes from record labels, even if the zine covers another topic. Since the history of zines is so intertwined with indie music, that has always been the advertising staple. There are other sources, however. If you want to solicit advertising try:

- Local retailers who carry the items you cover. Of course, this only works if you distribute locally.
- Comics companies. They understand zines because many of their artists start out by self-publishing.
- Companies that produce the item you cover.
- Snowboard or skateboard companies. These are subcultures whose members read a lot of zines.

> Since the history of zines is so intertwined with indie music, that has always been the advertising staple.

How a Zine Differs from a Magazine

With regard to advertising, the primary difference between a fanzine and a magazine is that the latter is run like a business, which guarantees certain things, including: the exact date when a publication will hit the streets; that an agency verifies their circulation; and ad placement. For instance, a magazine may guarantee that two ads for the same type of product made by different companies will not be placed closer than a certain number of pages of each other.

Fanzines don't have to worry about these things. But there is another practice of the mainstream magazine biz in which *some* publications participate: running a positive story on a product if a company buys an ad. This type of corporate butt-licking, plus a compulsive need not to upset readers, is what necessitated the birth of fanzines in the first place. It's a good thing to keep in mind when the dollar signs start blurring your vision.

How One Person Does It

Since zines refuse to be bought out, the demands advertisers can make are much more negotiable. In the end, it is best to work only with people you respect; otherwise your zine transforms into "product," and God knows there is enough waste packing our landfills already. Here is how Jeff Smith runs the advertising end of *Feminist Baseball:*

"We tell people it comes out twice a year. I've done 15 in ten years, so that's about one-and-a-half a year. We solicit people and they approach us. We've done three or four issues with advertising. Most people that do ads that are still in business will keep doing ads. Three or four months before I publish, I send out a little ad circular and maybe I call a few of those people. I've been pretty lucky without having to harass people too much. I could probably get a little more advertising if I tried, but I get enough money to break even and maybe even make a little money. I'm not interested in having ads for stupid stuff."

One simple way to decide what advertising you will take is to divide it into mainstream and indie businesses; however, ask almost any band who has been on an independent label and they will tell you small businesses can be more cutthroat than major corporations. In some instances, it is a matter of survival, just like a publisher taking advertising to keep a zine afloat. In the end, the best option is to base your judgment on what someone wants to advertise, and whether or not you think he or she is a scrupulous person.

"Major [record labels] are sometimes more responsive because they have more money and more people working for them," says Smith. "You don't get lost in the shuffle . . . but there are no hard and fast rules. Majors tend to be nice because they pay you on time. If I get a record that I like, often I will send them a flyer. A lot of indies you've never heard of will write me for ad information. A lot of those labels exist in that nether world where you only know they exist if you get everything free in the mail."

THE ADVERTISER'S VIEWPOINT

OK—Just how do advertisers perceive zines? Well, here is one viewpoint: that of Carrie McLaren, who purchases advertising for the independent record label Matador and has recently resurrected her own zine, *Stay Free!* Since independent record labels grew alongside fanzines, they are a good, and often primary, source of advertising revenue. Does McLaren look for large circulation and glossy covers? No. She looks for honesty and an earnest approach.

"To be good, a zine has to do what they want and not kowtow to labels," says McLaren. "I look for people who put thought into what they are doing and don't just want free stuff. Circulation does not make a difference. If we want large circulation, we advertise in a glossy magazine. If someone wants us to advertise, they should send us a copy of their zine and ad rates if they have any. If we're interested, we'll call them. If they want to call us, wait a couple of weeks and call to see if we got it."

Fantagraphics, an underground comics company located in Seattle, Washington, buys advertising in zines as well. How they operate provides an excellent example of how small businesses outside the music industry view zines. "We have a really erratic advertising schedule so it is a case-by-case situation," says Chris Jacobs, director of promotions and marketing. "[A zine] has to mesh with our audience. If we're doing catalog ads, it depends on whether or not we like the zine. It is a really subjective thing. We advertise to just support zines we like—just because their advertising is cheap. Also zines have run ads of ours for free to lure larger advertisers. The most frustrating thing is people who just want comics advertising and are not familiar with us. You'd be surprised about how many people contact us and don't know what genre of comics we do."

SOME COOL THINGS

There are some cool things about advertising. First off, it's a nice way for someone to tell you he or she supports your project. Advertising also can help clarify just what it is that you hope to accomplish—challenge racism, sexism, or whatever battle you happen to be fighting—by publishing that kind of a zine. An excellent example of someone who uses advertising in this manner is Carla DeSantis of *ROCKRGRL*. She runs her publication like a magazine, yet holds fast to her ethics.

"I stopped selling the back page because I was using that for a mailing label and selling T-shirts and subscriptions. Now I have a tear-away card [for orders] on the back. I want *ROCKRGRL* to be subscription-driven. I still envision that people are getting something out of it besides advertisers selling condoms. It doesn't make sense from a business standpoint, but it makes sense from a purely altruistic point. I have someone who is selling ads for me now. I really feel that I'd like to make a dent with [music equipment] manufacturers

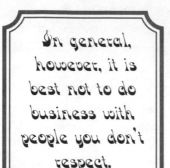

In general, however, it is best not to do business with people you don't respect.

who don't believe there is a market and don't advertise to women at all. I'd like to make a dent and get some of these [people] turned around. Our money is as green as anyone else's."

Now *that's* twisting the institution of advertising to meet your agenda. In general, however, it is best not to do business with people you don't respect. If you call someone and request that he or she buys an ad, know what he or she does. It's insulting to ask someone for money if you aren't familiar with the product. Most people who advertise with zines' are as passionate about their obsession as you are about your zine. It works both ways.

SPONSORSHIPS

If you can finagle one, a sponsorship is a fabulous way to help defray the costs of producing a zine. Sponsorships do come with their own set of complications, however. First off, you must present the potential sponsor with a proposal indicating how often you plan to publish and how sponsoring your zine will benefit him or her—and then you have to *deliver* what you promise. Sponsorships are similar to advertising. The main difference is that you only have one advertiser. This section outlines the elements of a proposal, includes an example of a sponsorship proposal for a zine serving a local film community, and suggestions on how to select potential sponsors.

Parts of a Proposal

A proposal serves two main purposes. It lets the potential sponsor know that you have a game plan, and convinces him or her that your zine will reach an audience of interest to him or her. The primary elements of a proposal include:

- Your vision for the zine;
- A rationale as to why your (proposal) zine would be of interest to your readers;
- A description of your zine's leadership and contributors;
- Where you plan to distribute your zine;
- An explanation of how the zine would benefit the sponsor;

- A summation of your long-term goals;

- A budget; and
- A mock-up of the zine.

What each of these sections should include and achieve is described below.

Vision

This section should describe what you plan to accomplish with a zine. It should answer the questions:

- How frequently will the zine come out;
- Who your audience is (a brief description);
- How many pages the zine will be;
- What format (type and size of paper) you plan to use;
- What the content will be;
- Any added benefits you plan to provide the community or advertiser. For example, if it is a music zine, you could cosponsor a show at a club with the company that is sponsoring your zine.

Rationale

This is a statement that explains why your zine needs to exist, and contains an expanded explanation of your potential audience and why they are not currently being served in an adequate manner. Remember to describe the audience in a way that will show the potential sponsor how helping your zine will benefit their company. For example, if you are doing a surf zine, indicate that, while national magazines do exist for surfers, there are no publications which keep the local community informed about what is happening in your region. This lets the sponsor know why people will pick up your zine and that your readers will purchase their product. Of course, you then have to choose an applicable sponsor. In this case, that would be a surfboard manufacturer or some related type of business.

Leadership and Contributors

In this section of the proposal, you need to let the potential sponsor know why you and your contributors are qualified to put out a zine. In order to get a sponsor, you need to have someone with publishing knowledge involved in your project. That experience could either be previous mainstream training or simply zine experience, but, if it is the latter, be prepared to send the potential sponsor some excellent copies of your staff's former ventures. The more information you can provide, the better your chances of receiving sponsorship. Try to detail as many of the following as possible:

- Who will be managing the project;
- Who will be designing the zine;
- Who the writers will be;
- Anyone else who has past experience in publishing and who will be contributing to the zine.

Distribution

Remember to include a listing of potential drop-off points for your zine in this section. You need to demonstrate how those distribution points will adequately reach your readers. For example, if you are putting out a zine on local designers, indicate that you will not only have your zine in various shops around town, but also at fabric stores and espresso stands where fashion victims hang out.

Benefits to the Sponsor

Although all the sections are designed to sell your zine to the sponsor, this one outlines precisely how sponsoring your zine will benefit their business. You must let the potential sponsor know:

- That a large proportion of your audience may purchase the sponsor's product;
- That you plan to help promote the company's product with events that they can sponsor through the magazine;
- The amount of space you will provide them to promote their product in the zine;
- How many people the zine will reach and the cost of reaching each of those people (cost per zine).

Long-Term Goals

This is a nebulous section, but it will demonstrate to potential sponsors that you are thinking long-term. Only you know what those goals may be. Do you want to be around for five years? Increase the number of pages in the zine? Go national? Have a glossy cover? It is also important to detail how you plan to achieve these goals. You must demonstrate that you have a long-term vision for your project.

Budget

Providing a budget lets the sponsor know that you will be around three months after the first issue comes out. It shows the sponsor that you can think fiscally, which is necessary if you want someone else to fund your project. At a minimum, a budget should include printing and distribution costs.

> At a minimum, a budget should include printing and distribution costs.

Mock-Up

This section provides an example of the zine you're planning, and indicates what will go where in it, including the sponsor's ads.

FINDING A SPONSOR

Sound more like a magazine than a zine? Well, it's close, but magazines have advertisers, not sponsors. Money for sponsorships is also generally funneled through the marketing rather than the advertising department of a business. Sponsorships are for people who plan to put out a specific type of zine long term. If you want to do something spontaneously, this is not the way to go. A sponsorship is a business agreement you enter into to do what you want, to put out a zine. Like any good business arrangement, it has to be based on respect. Don't accept sponsorship from someone you dislike or disagree with in any way. It will result in disaster.

The key to getting a sponsor is approaching the right type of business. It is essential to find someone who would benefit from sponsoring your zine. The people who read your zine must be likely to buy what your sponsor sells. In some cases this is simple: A zine about natural healing could approach a company which produces herbal medicine. In other cases, the opportunities are not so obvious. If you put out a zine on gambling, perhaps an airline would sponsor your zine. It takes some brainstorming. Ask the question: What type of products do the people who read your zine consume? The following example is of a proposal to a props shop requesting they fund a zine for the local film industry.

Sample Proposal
(Proposal for <u>Take 2</u>)

Vision

To produce a free, monthly, eight-page tabloid zine with a four-color cover on newsprint which serves the Northwest film community and film fanatics. The zine will contain the following:

- A listing of upcoming casting calls and openings for work in the Northwest film industry;
- Interviews with key people on what they look for in the people they hire to work on their films;
- Interviews with people who have worked on specific films;
- A "hints" section.

The zine also will provide added benefits to the community, including industry workshops.

Rationale

The Northwest currently has no publication which serves the thriving freelance film community. *Take 2* will provide individuals with a way to network within the film community. While *Media Inc.* covers what is being filmed in Washington State, it does not cover Oregon, nor does it let people know what work is available. National magazines also serve this audience, but they fail to address the primary concern of the region, which is the fluctuation in the availability of work. The Northwest film industry is growing, yet it is not stable. It is fertile ground for a community zine which helps draw people together. The sponsor of this zine will gain community loyalty. *Take 2* would also increase awareness of your props shop among people who work in the business and thus bring in more business, not only through readership of the zine, but also by word of mouth.

Leadership and Contributors

The zine will be edited by Jane Filmfreak, who is currently the critic for a major metropolitan newspaper *[you would want to include the name of the paper here]*. In addition, Guy Filmfreak, a local graphic artist and film editor who has worked on *[include names of projects],* will design the paper.

[Note: When writing an actual proposal, you should include clips of both people's work in this section.]

Distribution

Take 2 will be distributed throughout the Northwest at costume and supply stores, bookstores with extensive film sections, post-production shops, and schools with film departments. It will also be handed out at premieres and any parties involving the film industry.

Benefits to the Sponsor

Since the Northwest film community is in great need of a publication of this kind, sponsoring *Take 2* would enhance the community acceptance of any business. Additional benefits include:

- A targeted market (the Northwest film community) that is otherwise hard to reach;
- Word-of-mouth awareness among people who work in the film industry;
- The awareness of regional film buffs who read trade publications;
- One page of advertising in each paper, and the ability to reach 5,000 people at a cost of $.44 each;
- Discounted ads when the zine opens its doors to advertisers;
- The ability to sponsor local events to help the Northwest film community grow. You would catch people as they enter the business.

Long-Term Goals

Take 2 will grow with the film industry in the Northwest. After three years of sponsorship, it will open up to advertising. This will allow it to expand in size. Naturally, the initial sponsor will be given preferred placement of advertising and a substantial discount.

Budget for Take 2

<u>Annual Budget</u>

Startup Costs

Computer	$2,500
Printer	1,500
Fax machine	300
Scanner	600
Computer programs	2,995
Total	$7,895

Office

Two phone lines and long distance	$2,000
Supplies	1,200
Total	$3,200

Distribution

Vehicle rental	$2,000

Printing (5,000 copies, 8 pages)★

Printing	$6,000
Two full-color pages	6,500
Misc. printing costs	1,000
Total	$13,500

Grand Total	$26,595

★Additional process color pages available for $6,500 annually or $3,250 for a six-month period.

Mock-Up

cover 1	*sponsor ad* 2	*industry interview* 3	*industry interview continued* 4
interview with someone who has worked on a recent film 5	*hints section* 6	*list of casting calls and work opportunities* 7	*back page sponsor ad* 8

ADVERTISING VS. SPONSORSHIPS

Both advertising and sponsorships have their benefits and drawbacks, but between the two, advertising is definitely the easier way to go. However, if you plan to put out a zine on a regular basis for a specific audience, you can get most of your costs covered by a sponsor. The only drawback is you have to publish when you say you are going to and the sponsor ads have to look *good* (of course, *all* ads should look good but it doesn't hurt to proof sponsor ads extra carefully and have them approved prior to publication).

For a fun project, try doing it on your own. It's much less of a headache. If you want to grow or improve, the options of advertising and sponsorship will always be there.

CHAPTER FIVE
THE ART OF PRODUCTION

*a*bove all else, it is important not to go too high-tech when you start producing your zine. Use what you have. For some people that will be the word processor at work, for others the computer system at school. There is always the tad-too-expensive option of Kinko's, or, alternatively, you can take a PageMaker® class at your local community college or voc-tech school. This will teach you the basics of how to lay something out (some of which you should ignore), and, more importantly, provide you with access to the computer lab! But if you only have an ink pen and a copy machine, that will do.

The primary components of production include:

- Type;
- Rules;
- Art, including photographs.

And three ways of producing these elements are:

- Traditional—pen and paper;
- Pasteup;
- Computer design.

THE OLD-FASHIONED WAY

All you need to put out a zine is a good pen, some paper, and a photocopy machine. If you want to get fancy, shell out a few bucks for design tape (clear press-to-stick tape with either lines, type, or some sort of decorative border—hearts, stars, squiggly lines—printed on it in black). For your initial investment, you'll need a hard-tipped felt pen, a ruler, and paper.

TYPE

You don't even need a typewriter to publish a zine, although you can most certainly use one. If your copy is handwritten, make sure your writing is legible. Hard-tipped, narrow, felt-tip pens (like Sharpie®) provide clean lines. Also, remember to leave enough space between your letters so they don't garble together, and make sure there is an adequate amount of space between the lines.

Rules

Look at almost any publication and you'll see something called a "rule," a black line separating stories or comprising boxes around ads. Before the day of computer design, design tape made it easy for pasteup artists to create those lines. Design tape is something everyone should explore. It's still great stuff, especially for a kitsch effect. Felt-tip pens and a straight-edge are also great for creating your basic black line.

Artwork

For artwork, you have several options. Anyone who has seen a photocopied zine knows that most photographs look muddled at best. It's part of traditional zine style, but many publications, especially those carried at retail outlets, have moved past that. The reason for muddled photographs lies in a copy machine's inability to determine shades of gray. So, if you plan to photocopy your zine, make the limitations work for you:

- Consider utilizing *line art*. It reproduces well on a photocopier and, since the images are black and white, you can add a lot of detail.
- Use photographs for style and effect rather than as a staple.
- Remember black-and-white photos tend to reproduce better than color and that there is nothing to keep you from enhancing the delineation with the help of a felt-tip pen. The more contrast in the picture, the better the photo will reproduce.
- Clip art from other sources. Usually, this is illegal. Unless something is in the public domain (in other words, if it does not have a copyright) you are stealing. If you take something off a box, out of a magazine, or from a book or catalog, chances are either the artist or the corporation who put out the product owns the image.

But there's still plenty of stuff you can use and lots of ways of using it. Even art directors at hip magazines steal. One way to make something your own is to blow it up, shrink it, cut it up, or mutilate it in some unique fashion. When photocopying, remember that clean, clear lines and high contrast produce the best results. Experiment with various types of images on a photocopier. You'll quickly get a feel for what works and what does not.

COVERS

One of the most important elements to any zine, photocopied or not, is the cover. Spend time on it. It should possess at least two things: the name of the zine and something to make people want to pick the zine up. Examples include interesting design; a descriptive cut-line explaining the zine's philosophy, theme, or content; or a list of stories or authors in the zine.

Usually, zines look best if the cover is on heavier stock than the internal paper. Thick construction paper works well—it can be photocopied, or you can customize each copy.

> Usually, zines look best if the cover is on heavier stock than the internal paper.

Color, collage, or sparkle the covers, whatever you want. With a small production run, doing the cover can be fun.

PASTEUP

The next level of sophistication is manual design, or pasteup. Even though, in the long run, buying the materials to do manual design will cost more than buying the computer and software that perform the same process, it's an archaic but fun form. The tools include:

- A computer and word-processing system;
- Razor-blade knives, such as X-acto® knives;
- A waxer and the accompanying wax;
- Design tape such as Chartpak™ art;
- White tape—to cover up mistakes;
- A scanner or access to halftones;
- Flats, pieces of stiff cardboard with grids on them to help you place elements (halftones, copy, art) that make up pages.

Because it's hands-on, this method is more fun than designing on computers. It feels more like doing real art. The initial steps are simple: Take the type (copy, story). Wax it on the back, then slap in on the page—along with the art, which is also waxed.

TYPE

Not only does a word-processing system allow you to make changes and corrections quickly, a good program (like Microsoft Word®) will allow you to use various fonts (type styles), alignments—flush left, flush right, or centered—and column breakdowns. In other words, you can have the copy flow straight across the page or be broken into a series of columns. You can also produce the same effect on your own by setting narrow, justified margins on your computer and simply pasting more than one column on a page.

WAXERS

A waxer is an amusing device which consists of a roller and container into which you put chunks of wax to melt. The melted substance is rolled onto the back of the galleys (strips of paper containing type) and then the galley is pressed onto the flat. If you purchase a waxer, make sure to read the instructions carefully, as waxers are easy to destroy in innocent ways. The most common mistake is to run them back and forth over a piece of paper as if you were ironing. They should only be rolled in a forward motion, otherwise they will eventually leak. Using wax, rather than glue or tape, allows you to pull up the paper from the flat without ripping it. It takes practice to line paper up on those grids! Wax also allows you to play with other elements of the design—like where to place photos or headlines. If you don't like the way something looks, simply pull it off and place it somewhere else.

HALFTONES

Halftones are pictures that have been specially processed so that when they are printed they come out clearly. The half-tone process converts a photo with its continuous flow of tones into a series of dots. Since printing is done in layers of dots (the process is explained in Chapter 8, page 94), halftones produce a clear image, because the picture is compatible with the printing process. This is an archaic form being replaced by computer technology, but often halftones look better than computer scans (which will be described later). If you have access to the equipment and can learn how to make your own halftones, do it. It's worth the effort. The other option is to take your photos to a pre-press service facility (look in the phone book).

A few items to remember regarding halftones:
- Don't waste your money trying to halftone a muddy picture; use a photo that has contrast, or employ some other type of art. It's a great service, but only if you start with a good photo.

- If the photo is clear but the halftone comes back muddy or with not enough contrast, ask the pre-press plant why. If they can't provide you with a good reason, insist that they do it over at no charge. A good place will do that for you.

- Eventually, you will know what to expect from halftones and when a photo will come out the way you have in mind.

Scanners

The scanner, with the help of a computer, translates an analog image (something that is continuous, like the flow of watercolors or colors in a photograph) into dots and creates a digital image. Since each scanning program works differently, it is necessary to thoroughly read the instructions that come with both your computer system and scanner in order to get the best effect. Scanners are a bit pricey. If they are out of your range, you can have scans made at pre-press shops. Make sure they print out at least two copies. Sometimes they rip.

Color

You can use two different methods of color—spot and processed. Here's the scoop:

- **Spot color** is simple. You tell the printer where you want a particular color on a page (on headlines and in boxes, for example), and he or she will print the indicated items in a color other than black. The printer basically applies the color where you want it. You can also print a percentage of a color, so it appears lighter (see Chapter 8, page 100).

- **Process color** is a bit more complicated. If you want to print color photographs, you have to use process color. However, process color can be used to print *any* color or combination of colors. To proof the artwork which will appear when the zine is printed, you can order a color separation where each of the four colors used in process printing (cyan, magenta, yellow, and black) is printed on a transparency. When laid over one another, the transparencies recreate the image. This allows you to correct mistakes (like orange skin) before they happen. You simply tell the printer what you want changed.

Printing with process color is complicated, not to mention expensive. Most zines will never do it. If you decide to venture into this area, taking a class on the process or having someone familiar with it tag along to the printer to teach you the ropes is highly recommended.

COMPUTER PRODUCTION

If you are starting from scratch, are interested in an economical form of production, and aren't into the actual art of production, computers provide the best option. This is not to say design on computers is not artistic—it can be. The trick is to not let the medium (in this case computers) limit you. Don't follow the design rules in the books, otherwise your zine will look like a corporate newsletter.

> Software also comes in combination packages that provide you with everything you need.

Computers provide a large range of graphic options including typesetting, layout, scanning, drawing, photo manipulation, and color production.

What types of programs you get depend on the type of computer you purchase. For the Mac, which is great for graphic design, the most common include PageMaker®, QuarkXPress®, Illustrator®, and Photoshop®. You also can get software that works strictly on IBM and IBM-compatible computers. Various hardware and software options will be addressed in the next chapter. Software also comes in combination packages that provide you with everything you need. Essentially, most graphic software programs are similar. They just work at different levels of sophistication.

THE BASICS

To start publishing on a computer, you need at least a basic word-processing program and a design program. Make sure the first is compatible with the second, because you will need to electronically transport your edited copy from your word-processing program into your design program (for example from Word® to PageMaker®).

Although this book addresses the functions of various programs, it does not provide instructions on how to use specific ones. The truth is, after learning the basics, the most successful designers learn by experimenting. There are various different ways to learn those basics. It might be enough to run through the tutorial which is sometimes provided along with the software. In other cases, tutorials are available at public libraries. Another option is to attend classes at community colleges (private ones tend to be pricey). Purchase how-to books on desktop publishing for your particular system. Assuming you know the *primary* purpose of a word-processing system—typing—the new mystery is design software. Design software usually mimics manual layout by providing a pasteboard (see example of a QuarkXPress® layout below).

You can match the dimensions of your pasteboard to the size of your zine by defining the dimensions on the "master page," in your program, which will then produce a series of pages meeting your requirements. The options available in layout software vary dramatically and can include the ability to:

- Import various programs (word processing, drawing, photo manipulation, scans);
- Detail typesetting commands;
- Specify spot colors;
- Perform pre-press routines like trapping; and
- Make color separations.

TYPESETTING TERMS

Unless you have experience in design or printing, chances are terms like "trapping," "color separations," and "spot color" are unfamiliar, so here are some basic definitions:

Fonts: Type styles.

Kerning: The spacing between letters and words. If two letters appear to be jammed together tightly (or "crash"), you can increase the kerning.

Leading: The spacing between the lines.

Style sheets: An automated way to format text. They enable you to easily indicate the type style and face in which specified text should appear.

Typesetting: The ability to manipulate type in terms of fonts, kerning, style, and leading. Most word-processing programs can only change fonts and, to some extent, style—they can't control page design.

DESIGN TERMS

Airbrushing: Retouching artwork with color. Traditionally, this was done with a small hand-held sprayer. Now you can do it in a computer program.

Clip art: Art that can purchased in large books or on computer discs. In fanzines, it is often taken from other sources, such as old books or magazines.

Color separation: The process of separating the colors of an image into cyan (blue), magenta, yellow, and black filters (film) which can be laid on top of each other so the publisher can see approximately how the printed product will look.

Color transparency: A fancy name for a color slide. They range in size from 35 mm to 8 x 10 inches.

Contrast: Refers to the difference between light and dark tones in an image, including their relationship to one another within the image as highlights, middle tones, and shadows. You can manipulate this in most graphic programs.

Cropping: Cutting off part of an image.

Dot area: The proportion of a given area that is taken by a halftone dot (visual example provided).

Dot gain: The difference between the dot which appears on the film (in a color separation) or in an original copy, and the finished product. The way ink is absorbed by various forms of paper makes a difference. Glossy paper has very little dot gain, while newsprint has a high absorption rate. Too much dot gain causes letters or images to blur and become indistinguishable.

Halftone: An image made up of a series of dots which reproduce it. The dots vary in size.

Importing: Transporting elements such as type and art from one program to another.

Matte: Not glossy; a dull paper surface or photographic finish.

Scanner: A machine that creates an electronic image of a photo or printed document, in either color or black and white. When printed, the result is similar to that of a halftone.

Spot color: A single color added to the printing process. In other words, it is not processed and does not involve color separations like a color photograph. When you see a zine with a splotch of bright red on the cover, it is using spot color.

Text flow: The manner in which the text flows. This can include across the page, as well as from one column to the next.

Text wrap: The manner in which text wraps around an image.

Trapping: Proper trapping ensures that the (very small) area between different colors being printed receives the proper amount of ink from each.

Now that you are thoroughly intimidated by the lingo, know that unless you venture into fairly sophisticated printing, you probably won't encounter these items. Even if you do, learning them can be fun. Just use the same approach as Jeff Gilbert, publisher of *Mansplat*.

Gilbert produces *Mansplat* in the second bedroom of his apartment using a Macintosh computer, a laser printer, and a scanner. He downloads his imagery from the Internet, manipulates it in a program called Photoshop, and designs his zine on PageMaker®.

> *Photo manipulation programs are fun since they permit an artist to alter reality.*

"I have one room where I do *Mansplat*," he says. "I can sit in there for 12 hours and dink around. I had all this software, so *Mansplat* was really just an excuse to learn how to use it. It's a good way to learn, because instruction manuals are written in such computerese. When you [teach yourself how to maneuver the programs] for a fanzine you just go in there and fool around for fun and [the programs] are actually really easy to use."

ADDITIONAL TOOLS

Other tools include programs that allow you to draw, and to manipulate photos. Drawing programs include a series of tools that let you create shapes and add special effects with your mouse. Most also let you import items from scanners and include a photo manipulation application so you can trace or enhance images. Some are also equipped to import text and allow you to forgo a graphics program altogether, although that would be most appropriate for design-driven zines. Photo manipulation programs are fun since they permit an artist to alter reality. They allow you to add things that weren't originally there and to touch up photos.

E-ZINE GRAPHICS

E-zines are inherently different in appearance from paper publications; therefore it's important to work within the medium and use it to its full advantage. One often hears designers who prefer to work with traditional materials (design tape and razor-blade knives) whine that everything on the Web looks like it was produced by a hack; however, creativity is never limited by a medium. Rather than trying to mimic the appearance of a paper zine, bend technology to your advantage. On-line zines trade funky familiarity for high-tech geekism when it comes to appearance. Finally, if you decide to put your paper zine on-line, take time to design the page specifically for the Web. Nothing is more boring than scrolling through endless copy on a screen, no matter how entrancing the content is.

Graphics in an e-zine are created by loading in images and using tables which outline areas on a page into which you can put text or graphics. Depending on the browser you have, the table will be presented as anything from a black box to a textured area. You can also create rules and lines. Since graphics take a long while to download, it is important to use them well and with discretion.

"The idea is to make your graphics take up the least amount of memory possible because when people access them on the Web they're going through a modem," says Michael Cox, publisher of the *Music, Coffee, and Baseball* home page. "If you've got a page-sized graphic, a person could go have lunch and come back before it's done downloading. You've got to have your graphics as easy to load as possible. First, you don't want them to be too large in physical dimension. Second, you want to format them in a way that minimizes the size of a graphic. But remember, graphics are what attracts a reader to a page, just like they do in a fanzine or magazine. People are attracted by what's on the page and you keep them interested by having good content."

While these are all great toys, it is important to remember they are expensive and not necessary. Art clipped from old magazines, health books, or encyclopedias helps create great design. A zine produced on your kitchen table with felt-tip pens and printed on a copy machine has no lesser value than one designed on computer and printed in full color on expensive paper stock. It's the ideas that count.

Chapter Six
EQUIPPING YOUR NEEDS

f your vision of a zine involves hammering out copy on a typewriter or word-processing system at work or school, you can skip this chapter and return when you plan to purchase some nasty computer gear. Otherwise, welcome to hell. Since it tends to be somewhat of a major investment, purchasing computers and software is a headache. For a complete setup, the basics include a computer, scanner, printer, and software. This chapter will give you an idea about where to start with all these elements.

COMPUTERS

You can purchase two different types of computers, a Macintosh or an IBM (sometimes called a PC). Clones (basically knockoffs) of each version also are available. Traditionally, the graphics industry has used Macs; however, most programs designed for Macs now are available in an IBM-compatible format. If you're starting from scratch, Macs and Mac-clones cost more, but are generally considered more user-friendly.

If you've worked with IBMs, you are familiar with those funky, secret languages used to run them. Software designed for Macs is based on icons, making working on them a bit like playing a board game. Since the advent of Microsoft Windows®, working on IBM (and said clones) has become a lot more like working on Macs, but you still have to type in the occasional command.

Before you launch a shopping spree, the first step is to decide what programs you want to run, as well as how much storage space you will need to produce your zine. If you only plan to typeset copy, almost any model will do; however, those who use a lot of graphics and plan to completely design a fanzine on their computer need to make sure the hardware they purchase can run the programs they want.

Graphics absorb a lot of RAM (memory), to run programs, and hard disk space to store designs, graphics, and other files. So, make sure you purchase a computer with enough RAM. Here's how to figure out what you'll need:

- Determine what software you will use.
- Find out how much RAM is required to run each program.
- Figure out what software needs to run simultaneously.
- Add together the amount of RAM required for the separate programs which will run simultaneously. That is the minimum amount of RAM you need.
- Purchase a computer with significantly more RAM than the maximum you anticipate using because not only will you inevitably upgrade, but you'll also find new software you just have to have.

The amount of hard disk space you need is a bit tricky to figure out. It all depends on how complex your designs are, as well as on the type of graphics you use. Luckily, you can purchase an infinite amount of external memory (the same type of memory contained on your hard drive but stored in a box you attach to your computer). The benefit of external memory is that you can use it to upgrade your next computer. You can never have too much (or sometimes it seems even enough) memory.

When you purchase your first computer, consider buying a used one. You can peruse the classified section of the newspaper or go on-line, but a better option might be a broker, as they check out and sometimes will even warranty their merchandise.

SCANNERS

The world of scanners grows more complicated every day. It used to be you just popped an image onto the scanner bed and hoped for the best. Since there are now an array of options, it is important to know how scanners work so you can purchase the one that best suits your needs.

Here's how they work: An analog (something that is continuous, like the flow of watercolor, or colors in a photograph) image is placed onto the scanner bed. The scanner then reads the image and the computer then transforms the picture from an analog to a digital (dot) image, in a process much like that for producing a halftone.

When purchasing your scanner, pay special attention to the *dpi* (dots per inch). Those who plan to print on newsprint need a low dpi. But if glossy paper is in your plans, find a scanner with a high

dpi. Some scanners allow you to adjust dpi with software; however, it is best to purchase something that meets your needs to start with. To make sure you get what you need, bring in an image and have the salesperson print it out as interpreted by the scanner. Keep in mind that the computer, program, and printer you use will also affect the final image. Also, consider the size of the *scanning surface*. You want the scanner to be able to catch the full image you want to reproduce, not cut off the top of someone's head. Those who plan to work with large pieces of art need a scanner with a large bed (surface).

PRINTERS

In most cases an ink jet printer will work—as long as the ink cartridge is full—but be aware that laser prints are always better since they produce crisper images. If you output your zine on someone's else's printer, you'll have to make sure that their computer contains all the fonts and can open all the programs you require, and that you may have to set up the margins and tabs to match your document when printing out word-processing documents. After going through all that trouble, you may find that a $300 printer is a good investment. Like everything else, you can buy them used.

> *After going through all that trouble, you may find that a $300 printer is a good investment.*

SOFTWARE

There's a wide variety of graphic software, so we'll look at the basic players—Microsoft and Adobe. Like computers and printers, software can be purchased used. If you're going to go with an IBM or IBM clone, invest in Windows '95®, but make sure your computer has the RAM necessary to run it! Along with that, purchase Word for Windows. It will provide you with most of the necessary operating systems. Word is also available for a Macintosh. This is probably the easiest and most advanced word-processing system around and has been for years. With any experience in word-processing software, you can learn Word for Mac with almost no effort. After that refreshing word of comfort, let's move to the more complicated software.

MICROSOFT

Microsoft produces a "lite" desktop publishing system called Microsoft Publisher®. It's simple, and will provide what is needed to put out a basic zine. It can also be enhanced with design packs including the Original Version, Special Occasions, and Styleline. These are designed to create newsletters, so, if you go this route, take extra care to ensure your zine doesn't look like a local church flyer.

The packages provide the following features:

- Microsoft Publisher®, which is compatible with most major word-processing systems, provides examples of how to lay out your zine (or in their world, a newsletter) by providing standard designs; it contains 20 fonts (different types of lettering); has the ability to manipulate type—slant, stretch, and curve; and includes clip art.
- Original Version Design Pack, which includes Microsoft Draw®; this provides borders and supplies clip art.
- The Special Occasions Design Pack is slanted more toward making invitations and greeting cards than designing publications, but, for the record, it contains 30 additional borders, 200 more clip art images, and something called Styleline Design Pack—another 200 pieces of clip art, some of which are wonderfully kitschy.

ADOBE

When it comes to design, Adobe products are like a toy chest. Unfortunately, it's a pricey toy chest built around PageMaker®. If you have an IBM computer, you can use later versions of PageMaker® with Microsoft Windows®. Adobe products that you might consider include: PageMaker®, Photoshop®, Gallery Effects®, and Illustrator®. Some of their capabilities overlap, and although Photoshop®, Gallery Effects®, and Illustrator® are fun toys, one can design a zine on a computer with just PageMaker® and a compatible word-processing system.

PageMaker® reads text from numerous word-processing systems, and includes a Pantone color library to help you select which inks you want to use on your publication. Probably the best feature of PageMaker® is the ease with which you can put it to use. Here is what the program will do for you:

- Place text;
- Crop images;

- Re-size images;

- Rotate images;
- Wrap text around images;
- Make color separations;
- Create trappings (a process defined in Chapter 5, page 71);
- Assign spot color;
- Word process, although the system is somewhat slow;
- Magnify images;
- Lock objects into place;
- Align design elements automatically;
- Move groups of items;
- Send an item to the back so you can manipulate another element without having to move the first one.

Photo Options

Photoshop® and *Gallery Effects*® permit a designer to retouch, manipulate, and texture photos. People with photography experience will benefit most from Photoshop®, and those with an art background will have the best luck utilizing Gallery Effects®; however, that type of experience is not necessary for either program.

With *Photoshop*® you can make a horrible photograph acceptable, as well as alter the apparent light sources in a photo. The program allows an artist to manipulate an image by adding textures or patterns and to retouch a photo by smudging, blurring, or sharpening the image. It allows the fantasy-driven to create composites of various images, not to mention rotate and stretch a picture, and in addition provides the ability to:

- Correct color and retouch photos;
- Increase or decrease saturation;
- Lighten or darken an image;
- Correct an exposure (to some extent);
- Saturate and desaturate color;
- Do airbrush effects;
- Detect colors that are out of gamut (unable to print on a press);
- Adjust ink saturation on the various plates which deposit the colors during the printing process (this process is detailed in Chapter 8, page 94). This feature allows you to get a specific color, or prevent some of the color accidents that happen during the printing process.

Gallery Effects® is broken into three volumes which help an artist **77** further manipulate photos by providing tools which mimic art supplies, including palette knives, brushes, pens, and colored pencils. It can make something appear as if it's painted on canvas or on a piece of stone. Essentially the program transports an image to another location or form. Adobe Illustrator® is a program consisting of drawing tools. It allows you to draw images and paint them with a somewhat less sophisticated system than that used in Photoshop®. The typography system lets you adjust kerning, tracking, and point size, as well as wrap text around images. You can also bend type and images.

> Some people call them e-zines, but let's face it, on-line zines are simply Web pages, and they are, by nature, different from real zines....

You can purchase relatively inexpensive substitutes for both Photoshop® and Gallery Effects® as well. Adobe makes *PhotoDeluxe®*, which is a "consumer" program that allows you to fix basic photo problems—like those satanic, red dots that appear in people's eyes. You can get it for under $100; Photoshop® costs more than $800. Like Photoshop®, Gallery Effects® also has a cheaper cousin, *SuperPaint®*, a program that allows the user to paint, draw, and process images in either black and white or color. Adobe also makes a slew of other products designed to create specific effects, including *Dimensions®*, to create a 3-D effect; *Adobe Font Folio®*, which provides more than 2,000 typefaces; and *Type On Call®*, which allows a designer to buy up to 2,000 typefaces by calling a line and purchasing a code; the fonts can be delievered on the Internet.

Once again, you can purchase most of these items used and reduce your costs significantly. Jeff Gilbert, publisher of *Mansplat,* used this method. "I used *Mansplat* as an excuse to buy all that stuff, at least that's what I tell my accountant," laughs Gilbert. "Everything I have is really cheap but it works well. I bought a scanner for $350. The most expensive thing I bought was the laser printer, which cost me about $1,500."

E-ZINES

 Some people call them e-zines, but let's face it, on-line zines are simply Web pages, and they are, by nature, different from real zines—

those charming chunks of paper with the bent corners and content. Still, if you have access to the hardware and software necessary to create a Web page, e-zines can be cheaper to produce than their paper counterparts. You just have to accept the possibility that some Internet supplier censor will deem your content too titillating, bleep your hours of hard labor from existence, and cancel your account.

SELECTING A SERVICE

Hands down, the most important factor in creating an e-zine is selecting the right service provider, or server. First off, make sure the package you select provides you with space for a Web page. Second, choose a local company instead of a large corporate carrier. They are less likely to censor your content, for both ethical and financial reasons; for one thing, a small on-line service probably does not have the manpower to monitor all its accounts for devious material. This will not, however, stop the local police department from perusing your site and taking note of your off-kilter comments.

Basically, services are divided into two categories: commercial, and personal use. If you do not plan to accept advertising and want a fairly small page, purchase a personal account. They start at about $20 a month. Most people will want a commercial account. They cost a bit more and benefits vary from service to service but usually include the following:

- The right to accept advertising.
- Additional space which allows you to put more images and graphics on your page.
- The opportunity to select your own *domain name*. To select a name you first need to do a search to see that the name is not already taken. You can do this through InterNIC located at http://rsinternic.net. Simply type up the name you want to use. If nothing responds, you can register your handle for a fee of $50 a year.
- Multiple e-mail addresses.
- More traffic access to your Web site.

HTML

HTML is the computer language used to build Web pages. You don't need to know the codes in order to create you own site, but it helps. There are several ways you can use, or rather avoid using, HTML (the initials stand for hypertext markup language). They include:

- Using the language in a text editor, such as SimpleText.
- Using a converter in a graphics program.

"Most people don't know all the code," says Michael Cox, publisher of the *Music, Coffee, and Baseball* home page located at www.accessonecom/~michaelc. "Therefore, you have various degrees of help in writing code. It goes from things that are a cross between text editors, to code writing instruments where you type out the text you want, hit some buttons, and they will put the code you request on the page."

SOFTWARE

As far as the mechanics of creating a Web page, numerous books exist on the subject, as a jaunt to any bookstore located in a suburban mall will verify. You can also find programs both in software stores and on-line through shareware with which to format your Web page. Shareware is an interesting, egalitarian concept. It is a program developed by an amateur who places his or her program on-line, allows people to download and use it, and then requests users to send a payment if they like how the software works. If you decide to use shareware, be nice and pay the developer. It usually costs between $5 and $50.

"What someone should use depends on how comfortable they are with the ability to learn code," says Cox. "If you want to do something without thinking about code, then get something that lets you do it completely graphically. That way you can do everything visually and not have to think about it."

There are drawbacks to using graphically based applications, however. It can affect the order in which graphics and text appear on your screen. Ideally, you want the text to appear while the graphics download. That captures the reader's interest and prevents him or her from jumping to another site. Unfortunately, using a graphically based program without troubleshooting capabilities may result in a slow-loading page.

If you decide to purchase items from a retailer, a total system, including software, costs about $5,000 when purchased for Mac. Obviously, there are an infinite number of playthings to buy, but you can always revert to pen, paper, and copy machine. Make a list of what you want, buy a computer that can handle your wildest wishes, and add a word-processing system. After all, most people do not have legible handwriting, and hammering out copy on your mother's ancient typewriter is a pain. A word-processing system is all a lot of people use. Everything else is extra.

BUDGETS

t's hard to imagine putting together a budget for something you may think of as a hobby. However, fanzines can be an expensive pastime, and creating a budget will help you figure out what you can afford to do. Can you sustain a glossy cover? How many copies can you print? How much do you need to charge? All these questions will be answered ahead of time if you develop a budget. In this chapter, you will learn how to calculate the cost of putting out a fanzine, including startup expenses plus the costs of office supplies, production, distribution, and printing. We will also explain how to calculate the cost of purchasing copy and art, if you decide to pay for it. Finally, you'll learn how to calculate your cost per zine, which will enable you to determine how much to charge per zine—if anything.

STARTUP COSTS

Many people will have access to at least some of the items on the following list. Few people will have access to everything. That's OK. Unless you plan to put out a slick, computer-produced zine, you don't need everything. In fact, you may need nothing in this section. The list is provided solely to determine what you *might* need so nothing essential is left out when you develop a budget. Keep in mind that everything on this list can be purchased used, and some specifics on types of programs and makes of computer are detailed in Chapter 5, page 68. The basics for producing a computer-generated zine include:

- A computer with adequate RAM to run all the necessary programs and enough memory to store at least one copy of your zine. You can store back issues on floppy disks if necessary. Additionally, you can purchase external memory and, if your computer has the capability, install additional RAM to upgrade your computer's speed, as well as its ability to run multiple programs simultaneously.
- A printer. If you purchase a laser printer, it may cost as much as your computer. If you are willing to have your copy and images

look a tad fuzzy, you can purchase an ink-jet printer for around $350, new.

- A fax machine. If you purchase a new computer, it may come with fax capabilities. While this is an excellent way to receive information, you will inevitably find that you need to fax something not created on the computer. On those occasions, either scan the image into a computer, or utilize your local mail service.

- A scanner. These range wildly in price. If you purchase a scanner with color capabilities, it will set you back significantly. Gray-scale (black-and-white) scanners cost less. If you plan to work only with spot color, the latter is all you need. Gray-scale scanners start at approximately $300, new.

- Computer programs. You can purchase an almost infinite number of computer programs. But to produce a computer-generated zine, you mainly just need a design program and a word processing program. If you plan to scan images, purchase a photo manipulation program. Additionally, you may want to purchase a program which guards against viruses, as well as something that serves as an address book.

- A tape recorder.

- A waxer, if you're not doing strictly computer design.

- A telephone. You probably have one of these already.

OFFICE

Office expenses include the supplies you need to produce a magazine, and the costs for additional phone lines, long-distance phone calls, postage, pens, pencils, tapes for interviews, and all the odd outlays you may incur simply to maintain an office. Of course, if you put out a small zine, few of these things apply, but some of them will—you'd be surprised. No matter how simple your zine is, it's a good idea to budget at least $50 per issue just to cover office costs. A long-distance telephone interview can run $10, while an ink-cartridge refill for an ink-jet printer costs about $25. If you have a laser printer, a cartridge refill may put you back close to $100. Here is a laundry list of items to consider when budgeting for your office—or at least your office supplies and costs:

- Phone lines. How many do you need? Are you going to use your personal phone for everything, or do you need a separate line for your fax and on-line service?

- Long distance charges.
- Computer paper, envelopes, and labels.
- Pens and pencils.
- Copies.
- Film and development charges for photographs.
- Computer ink cartridges.
- Halftones.
- Postage.
- Design tape.
- Razor-blade knives.
- Wax for a waxer.
- Tapes.
- Computer disks.

STAFF

Staffing is probably a non-issue, but just in case your zine is wildly received by the masses and you want to make it bigger, here is how you pay freelancers:

- Freelance writers. Writers are usually paid by the word. To esti-
  mate how much it will cost to fill the pages of your zine:
  —Mock up stories, including design, on the pages you plan to fill
   with paid copy.
  —Count the number of paid words on all the pages.
  —Multiply the number of words by how much you plan to pay your writers per word. Obvious-ly, you need to toy with the amount you want to pay them. One cent is a good starting point. If you paid them one cent a word, a 1,500-word story would cost $15.

  > The cost per page will help you calculate how much you will pay freelancers per issue....

  —Divide the total (the number of paid words in your zine multiplied by the amount you plan to pay per word) by the number of pages you plan to print. This gives you your cost per page.
  —The cost per page will help you calculate how much you will pay freelancers per issue, even if the number of pages in your zine fluctuates.

—Here is the formula (See, that algebra class did pay off!):
  Number of paid words on all the pages (X)
  The amount you plan to pay writers per word (Y)
  The number of pages used to calculate the average (P)
  The average cost per page for copy (A)

$$XY/P = A$$

—Then use A and the actual number of pages per issue (p) to calculate the freelance costs for each issue.

$$A(p) = \text{freelance cost per issue.}$$

- Freelance copyeditors and proofers. Proofreaders and copyeditors are paid hourly, unless your friend does it for free.
- Freelance photographers and artists are paid per piece, with a premium paid for cover art. Since the majority of art in zines is borrowed from other sources or not paid for, the best way to budget for this is to set the amount you plan to spend for a certain size issue and stick to it. A simple way to do this is to pay only for the cover art. Or, you can budget for the amount of art you plan to purchase for a certain amount of pages. (For example, one piece of paid art per ten pages.)
- Cover design is another optional expense. Most people design their own covers. If you want national distribution in retail outlets, however, a spiffy cover might prove to be a good place to dump additional funds. Retailers want a zine to have a cover which will encourage people to pick it up. Only you know if you have the capability to do this on your own.

DISTRIBUTION

The cost of your distribution depends on how you do it. If you have a company distribute your zine for you, you'll need to calculate in the discount it gives retailers as well as the percentage it takes for itself, which will vary depending on what company you use. If you distribute through the mail, figure out how much it costs to mail each zine, and multiply that by your circulation. If your distribution is local, keep in mind gas costs, or, if you have a large run and no van, vehicle rental.

PRINTING

Because the cost of paper changes drastically and with little warning, printing costs are hard to estimate. The best you can do is get a bid, pad it (because there *will* be unexpected problems), and hope nothing extreme happens to change paper prices during the next year.

When selecting a printer, the first priority is always to deal with someone who communicates well. After you find several of those people, compare their bids and keep an eye out for secret costs. Below is an itemized bid for a zine and its translation.

Bid for *Take Two*
XYZ Printing, August 1, 1997

Description
- 8-page tabloid, black only.
- Includes blueline proof, quarterfold, and bundling.
- No bleeds, customer picks up papers.
- Publication arrives on disc, camera ready. Postscripting provided by XYZ.

Type Stock
- 35" 1 lb. Electrobright
- 35" 2 lb. Electrobright

Customer
Provides camera-ready disc with placed art

Printer
15 minutes of postscripting plus plates and presswork. Postscripting in excess of 15 minutes will be billed at $60/hr.

Price

	First 5000 Ms	*Additional 1000 Ms*
35" 1 lb.	$500	$100
35" 2 lb.	$600	$120

- Cost per 2 common, full-color pages plus key is $529
- Separation scans $150 apiece, film outputs $50 apiece★

Additional
There will be additional charges for the following: delivery, scan seps, film output, postscripting in excess of 15 minutes, bleeds, full and process color, halftones, and other corrections.

Terms
- Payment one week previous to printing unless otherwise arranged
- Overruns and underruns not to exceed 10 percent
- Quote viable for 30 days
- Rebids provided for deviations before printing.

- Description. This section details:

  —How many pages the publication will be (eight);

  —What the format is (tabloid);

  —What type of ink is provided—black only. The cost of any process color pages is added later;

  —What perks are included in the total price. These are things other printers might charge for separately. They include blue-line proofs (non-color proofs that let you check for mistakes before printing), quarterfolding (folding the paper in half), and bundling the papers;

  —What is not included in the bid; for example, trimming (cutting the nonprinted border off the paper), bleeds (printing colors outside the established border of the paper), and delivery;

  —The format in which the paper must be delivered to the printer; in this case, on disk. Nothing needs to be specified for traditional pasteup layout. The bid does, however, state that the printer will do the postscripting, a process which curves the edges of letters (computer letters are actually built out of squares).

- Type stock. This section explains what type of paper you will receive. If you are unfamiliar with paper types, ask your sales rep

> Plates and presswork are elements of the printing process— all printers supply them.

to provide you with examples and explain the benefits of each. Here we have bids for one type of paper in two different weights. Both weights are the same size, 35 inches. Heavier paper is always nicer. Think of the difference between copy machine paper and computer stationery! The stationery has a heavier weight. Electrobright is a type of newsprint that appears whiter than your standard dingy variety.

- Customer. This section reiterates what must be supplied to the printer: a complete disk with halftones and art in place. This means the images must be scanned into the document and delivered on disk, too.

- Printer. This recapitulates what the printer will supply; however, it sets limits by indicating they will only provide 15 minutes of postscripting. Plates and presswork are elements of the printing process—all printers supply them.

- Price. The way to dissect this section is as follows:
  —The first column indicates the price for 5,000 copies at each weight of paper.
  —The second column, titled "additional Ms," indicates the additional cost per thousand zines printed over the first 5,000.
  —The third line projects the cost for process color pages, which you buy in sets of two. You can't choose where they lie, however. When you select one page for color, you automatically receive the one that is "common" with it. For example, if you purchase the front page, you get the back page because it lies on the other side of the fold. Included in the cost ($529) for two common color pages is a color key (to check the color before it is printed). What needs clarification is whether you get a color key for each page, or simply for one page, since the word "key" is singular. In the "additional Ms" column, it indicates the cost per thousand of printing extra copies with color, since you have already paid for the processing.
  —The fourth line clarifies the other costs for producing process color, including color separations (called "scan sep") and film outputs (the actual separation).
  —The ★ indicates that if it takes more than 15 minutes to postscript your zine, they will charge you $60 an hour for that function. This is something to compare with other bids.
- Additional. This is a laundry list of items for which you will also pay extra. Some have been mentioned previously, others have not.
- Terms. This indicates things that are assumed by the printer:
  —You must pay up front, unless you make other arrangements. No doubt this involves a credit check.
  —Overruns and underruns will not exceed 10 percent. This means the amount you order may vary by 10 percent. If you order 5,000 zines, you may get 5,500 or you may get 4,500.
  —A quote is only good for 30 days.
  —If you do not meet the specifications of the bid, they will rebid the job before printing it.

A SAMPLE BUDGET

How do you boil all this down? Like any math problem, you do it one step at a time. Here is how I calculated a budget for a fanzine I plan to produce. Keep in mind, this is for an expensive zine which comes out on a regular basis. I plan to help defray the costs with sponsorships.

Annual Budget

Startup Costs

Computer *(purchased new)*	$2,500
Printer *(purchased new)*	1,500
Fax machine *(purchased new)*	300
Scanner *(purchased new)*	600
Computer programs	
(provided by a friend who constantly upgrades)	0
Total	$4,900

Office

One phone line	$480
Installation ($60) plus $35 a month in basic charges	
Long distance *($100 x 12 months)*	1,200
Supplies *(ink cartridges, pens, stamps, paper)*	996
Total	$2,676

Staff

Freelance costs	$6,000

The $6,000 figure was determined as follows:
   $100 per issue for proofing.
   12 issues x $100 = $1,200.
   $50 per page freelance writer's costs.
   8 pages x $50 = $400 per issue.
   $400 x 12 issues = $4,800
   $4,800 (annual freelance costs) +
   $1,200 (annual proofing costs) = $6,000

Photographers	300
($25 per issue for cover shot; 25 x 12 issues = $300)	
Cover design	600
($50 per issue; 50 x 12 issues = $600)	
Total	$6,900

Distribution

   Vehicle rental $1,800

      I need a van to distribute 5,000 copies
      of the zine throughout the state.
      Rental $150 x 12 issues = $1,800.

Printing

Printing	$6,000
(5,000 copies, 8 pages, *taken*	
from the previously provided estimate)	
Two full-color pages	6,500
Estimated misc. printing costs	1,000
(*postscripting, fixing mistakes*)	
Total	$13,500

Total Annual Costs   **$29,776**

Cost per Zine Calculation Using This Example

Annual Cost (A)	$29,776
Number of Issues (N)	12
Number of Copies (C)	5,000

$A/N = X$ (Cost per Issue);
   therefore, $29,776/12 = $2,481.33

X/C = Cost per Zine;
   therefore, $2,481/5,000 = $0.50 (rounded up)

Keep in mind, the above budget is for a pretty snazzy zine with a large circulation. Yet the cost for producing a copy of the zine is only $0.50 each. Additionally, this includes one-time startup costs which will not exist the second year. Another important item to remember is that budgets are only estimates. The costs of things change and you will have to modify a budget as real expenses are recorded. Still, producing a budget will provide a good idea of what can realistically be accomplished. Since zines don't come out on a regular basis, you can always take time to save your pennies for the next issue. Finally, anyone can put out a simple zine. Pen and ink and photocopies are not cost-prohibitive. It's the fancy trimmings which get expensive.

THE JOY OF PRINTING

Since you don't physically have to do the task, printing is the easiest part of putting out a zine—right? Wrong. The technology behind printing is complicated. Unless you're educated and experienced, this gives the printer the upper hand, and some might use it to their advantage. This chapter will introduce you to four types of printing (photocopying, printing with only black ink, spot color printing, and process color printing). However, nothing except experience will educate you properly. Some voc-tech or community colleges offer basic classes on the technical aspects of printing. If a zine is a more than a casual project, you might benefit from such a course. It will greatly reduce your learning curve and allow you to master the terminology used in the trade. In order to lessen the pain, we'll start with the simplest option—photocopies.

COPYING

There are lots of ways to procure photocopies. Machines at countless day jobs have produced many a zine (not that we're encouraging that). Of course, you could consider getting a job at a local copy shop and photocopying your zine between paying customers. In this chapter, we'll focus only on the legal options.

Getting a good quality copy is simple. Just find a copy machine with an adequate amount of toner, make sure the glass surface is free of scratches, and clean the glass with window cleaner, which should be available at the copy shop. Remember that when copying in volume, it is also possible to save some time and effort by having the shop employees copy your zine. They can collate, staple, and fold the paper to give it a nice, crisp seam, which is hard to do on your own.

If you have the staff copy and collate your zine and the quality does not meet your standards—if there are specks on the paper, for example—don't hesitate to ask that it be redone. Small copy shops may cut you a deal if they get to know you. Don't expect this type of treatment at a large chain, however. Regardless, once your circulation exceeds 1,000 copies, it's usually more cost effective to print your zine rather than have it copied.

Assuming you'll want to print your zine like a saddle-stitched book (folded down the middle with a staple or two in the spine), it's often helpful to arrange your page flats (originals) for the copier or printer as follows, to help guarantee they are printed in the correct order. Sometimes page numbers printed on the page just aren't enough.

cover 1	back 14
2	13
3	12
4	11
5	10
6	9
7	8

- Find a box large enough to hold two flats side by side.
- For the first layer, place the cover and the back page in the box face up. Note that the page numbers add up to the total number of pages in the publication plus one. For instance, if you have a fourteen-page publication, the page numbers are 1 and 14.
- Add subsequent layers using the same addition method. After the cover and back page, place pages 2 and 13 in the box. All the page combinations placed in the box should add up to the total number of pages in your publication plus one. See the diagram at right.

PRINTING

You can choose from three basic types of printing:

- One color, which usually means printing black ink on a white or light-colored paper stock.
- Spot color, which involves selecting colored inks to print in addition to black. You may decide you want bright red headlines and accents with black text, for example.
- Process color, which creates virtually the full visible spectrum of color by using only four different colors of inks applied in a special series of dot patterns. Process color is only necessary if you want to add realistic photographs or many colorful illustrations to your zine pages. A few well-placed spot colors may be sufficient to give your zine enough flair without the added expense of using process inks.

Photographs, illustrations, and diagrams give your zine interest, dimension, and polish. For the beginner, it is best to give your printer your original photos and/or artwork clearly marked with crop, sizing, and color information and let them scan and place your final images. The more information and instructions you can write down for your printer, the better your final job will turn out.

When the printer scans your images (illustrations or photos), they are converted into a series of dot patterns called **line screens** that limit the amount of ink placed on the paper as the image varies. It works like this:

- When using only black ink, your printer will create a halftone image that is comprised of hundreds of different-sized tiny black dots. The darkest part of the image will have very fat dots and the lightest part of the image will have very thin dots. To the naked eye, this creates a visual effect of a continuous black-and-white image.

- You also can give your image a little more flair by specifying a (spot) color other than black. Your printer will have a color swatch (sample) book that you can pick from. Be aware that most images will look slightly lighter and have a little less contrast when a spot color is substituted for black.

- For a more realistic effect, you can print your images in process color (also known as full-color or four-color). Process color printing gives the illusion of a full range of color by interweaving dots of cyan, magenta, yellow, and black inks (abbreviated as "CMYK").

> Photographs, illustrations, and diagrams give your zine interest, dimension, and polish.

The process may sound a little weird, but it works surprisingly well. Ask your printer to show you a CMYK dot pattern under a loupe or magnifying glass. You'll be amazed by how well different combinations and variations of cyan (light blue), magenta (hot pink), yellow, and black can represent so many different color hues.

BASIC COLOR THEORY

Thoroughly confused? That's OK, we had to start somewhere. In this section, some of this should start making sense. To begin with: How can you make a full range of color from only four colored inks, and just what are cyan, magenta, yellow, and black anyway? Don't bother running to your box of crayons. It won't help.

Perhaps we should start with a little explanation of how humans view colors. There are two systems: **subtractive color** and **additive color**. Additive color you probably learned about in kindergarten. "Yellow and blue make green." Right? The three primary colors—red, yellow, and blue—are additive. When you mix any two of these colors, you get the color between them in the rainbow. (Remember ROYGBIV? This helpful acronym stands for red, orange, yellow, green, blue, indigo, and violet.) Blue and red make purple, and red and yellow make orange.

Subtractive colors, on the other hand, create colors by filtering out one hue to create another. Colors opposite each other on a color wheel are subtractive. Adding cyan subtracts red, adding magenta subtracts green, and adding yellow subtracts blue.

Additive colors are not used in process printing because most presses require each dot of ink to print directly on a white or "clean" space of the paper. Inks simply do not adhere well to already-inked areas of the paper. With additive colors, in order to get green you would have to mix yellow and blue ink. On a press, therefore, you would have to print one color on top of the other. For example, you might run the paper through a yellow inkwell to pick up the yellow dot pattern and the yellow ink would dry on the paper. You would then run the same sheet through a blue inkwell to pick up the blue dot pattern. Unfortunately, a dry yellow dot overprinted with a wet blue dot usually creates a messy brown dot. This is also the case with most other additive color ink combinations—not a good solution.

Subtractive colors, on the other hand, can be printed side by side in a special inter-leaved dot pattern. When a particular hue, say green for instance, is required, the printer can simply run a lighter dot of magenta, green's subtractive hue. For example, if you have a process-color dot pattern of cyan, magenta, and yellow and you want it to look more green, you reduce the size of the magenta dots. If you want more red, you reduce cyan and if you want more blue, you reduce the yellow dot. At right is a graphic illustration of the how subtractive colors relate to the colors you see on a printed sheet.

Process colors (CMYK) print in a series of dotted screen patterns that create a special geometric shape called a **rosette**. If lined up properly (called "in registration"), no two colors will overlap each other. Instead they form little clusters of color that trick your eye into seeing a specific hue. The dot patterns are so small that your naked eye confuses them for one true color tone.

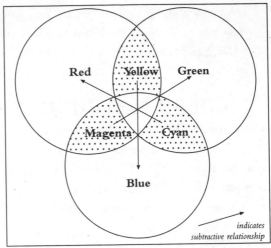

indicates subtractive relationship

"Okay," you say, "I'll take your word for it, but where does the black come in?" Well, adding more of all three colors in equal concentrations makes the dot pattern darker while reducing all three equally makes for a lighter tone. One hundred percent of cyan, magenta, and yellow creates an ugly brown, however, and that's why neutral black, the fourth color, is introduced as the overall color tone is darkened. Replacing equal parts of CMY with a percentage of neutral black (represented as a constant, K) in a dark image is called **under color removal**. Replacing lighter tones of CMY with a lighter screen of black (gray) to make a color more neutral or less brown is called **gray component replacement**.

PROCESS COLOR PITFALLS

There are also a variety of problems you can encounter with process color, the most common of which are moiré distortion and improper trapping.

- **Moirés** are one of the most common problems in printing. A moiré occurs when patterns of dots overlap or when the process color ink patterns are not lined up properly. With zines this problem typically occurs when you scan an image from another publication. The original set of halftone dots clashes with your set of printing dots. This results in a somewhat psychedelic, but unwanted, effect. If you are certain that your images are originals and you still see a subtle spinning pattern in your photographs, ask your printer to adjust the four-color plate registration.

- **Trapping** problems take place when two dissimilar colors "butt" up against each other and the printer has not adjusted the darker color to slightly "overprint" the lighter color. The most noticeable indicator of trapping problems is when you see white lines or white gaps between two color blocks that are supposed to touch each other.

COLOR MATCHING SYSTEMS

Color matching systems help guarantee that you receive the color closest to what you want. The most common is named Pantone Matching System (PMS), but a variety of others exist. Every printer uses some system. To effectively use a color matching system:

- Ask your print sales representative to provide you with a sheet of color options.
- Once you receive it, keep the key in a dark area, to prevent fading from sun exposure.
- Specify the colors by name on your cover letter when you order color from the printer. In other words, you wouldn't simply order "red," you would order "cherry red" or maybe "Pantone 1788 CV (red)."
- Remember a color matching system also lets you know what colors are out of the printer's *gamut* (range). In other words, what colors they cannot reproduce. The lack of a broad color gamut is not the fault of the printer, but rather a limitation of the technical process itself.

PAPER

The type of paper used can drastically affect the quality of your color and/or legibility of your copy and ads. There are two major categories of paper and many sub-categories. All paper can be divided into coated and uncoated stocks. Within these broad categories you can have alternatives like gloss coated versus matte coated or high-quality woodfree versus low-grade newsprint. There are various quality grades within each category as well. Further, your printer may have a "house stock," or a paper that costs less because the printer buys it in large quantities and stocks it for generic projects. Ask your printer for sample sheets to aid you in making your decision.

One can expect various effects or side effects from different types of paper. Below is a smattering of things to look for:

- **Coated paper–high-gloss finish**
  –Refracts light well and results in cleaner colors. The colors appear

dark, bright, and have a sheen. Any major fashion magazine is printed on high-gloss paper. Major national news magazines are also printed on glossy stock, but use a lower-quality paper.

–Has a low absorption level which results in less **dot gain.** It allows you to use smaller type and lines without having them blur.

- **Coated paper–matte finish**

  –Has more texture and therefore a lower gloss factor. Colors still appear true, but lack sheen. This is the type of paper on which most zines are printed.

  –Provides a moderate level of dot gain. Small type remains legible.

- **Uncoated paper–standard white**

  –Provides no gloss, so there is no sheen to the colors. The colors will also appear less bright.

  –Varies in level of brightness. Colors are slightly more intense but less detailed.

  –Has a higher level of absorbency, resulting in some dot gain. Small colored type may blur and become unreadable.

- **Uncoated paper–newsprint**

  –Provides no gloss, so there is no sheen to the colors. The colors will also appear less bright.

  –Varies in level of brightness but is always off-white. This results in colors that are slightly off even though you select them from a color matching system.

  –Has the highest level of absorbency, resulting in a great deal of dot gain. Small type may blur and become unreadable.

Stark white, high-gloss paper provides the best results. Unfortunately, this is out of the price range for most small publications, so buy what you can afford. Most low-cost, white paper will provide more than adequate results. In fact, once they achieve a high circulation, some fanzines switch to newsprint for financial reasons. It's much less expensive and allows you to increase circulation and reach more people.

PURCHASING PRINTING

This process involves a bit of phone work, but before you start, know what you want. One color? Process color? Halftones? Color separations? Some print shops provide all these services. Even then it may be more convenient and economical to have halftones and color separations prepared at an independent pre-press service bureau.

Expect to make a lot of phone calls to find the best deal and then keep in mind that if you decide on process color, customer service is crucial. It's usually better to pay a little more for a printer who can explain the process to you. If someone cannot communicate well over the phone, or if they simply don't return your phone call, skip to the next listing in the book. Or better yet, ask another zine publisher who he or she uses.

Printing in one color (black) or two color is relatively simple and, for runs between 1,000 and 5,000, the best deal can often be found at large discount processors. For small runs you can consider a printer who uses paper-based printing plates, which are relatively inexpensive to produce. They also wear out quickly, resulting in poor quality in runs of more than 1,000.

The printing process becomes less daunting with experience, but it never ceases to cause at least occasional frustration for every publisher. Printing encompasses the largest zine publishing expense and the one over which you have the least control and creative input. Consider it a necessary evil. Even though this chapter warns of unscrupulous vendors, nice folks are everywhere, and you may even find someone who supports your off-the-wall project. If you develop a good rapport with your representative, ask him or her to notify you if he or she has a surplus of specific paper sizes or odd-size remnants left from previous jobs. You can often get them at a discount. Who says the size and shape of a zine has to be consistent? Like any obstacle, if you learn the mechanics of the printing process, you can make it work for you.

GLOSSARY OF TERMS

To further aid you in your adventure in printing, here is yet another list of terms. You may need some of them to help decipher what your printer is trying to say some of the time.

Achromatic: Colors that have no hue, such as white, grays, and black.

Adjacent color effect: The effect a large area of color has upon another, smaller area of color. For instance, a large area of orange may make a small area of blue seem less bright.

Brightness: The reflective property of paper. Paper with more brightness reflects light better and therefore appears whiter and/or brighter.

Continuous tone: The variation of density in a printed image. If you see an image where the color varies where it should not, it has poor continuous tone.

Density: The ability of an ink to reflect light.

Desaturated color: A color that looks faded.

Dot area: The percentage of an area occupied by a halftone dot or line screen. In other words, a 50-percent dot area uses up half of its available space, while a 100-percent dot area uses it all.

Dot gain: The amount an ink spreads in excess of the defined dot area due to excess ink absorption by the paper. Dot gain is highest on porous papers like newsprint and lowest on high-gloss papers. You may request a 50-percent dot area and end up with a slightly higher percentage due to dot gain.

Four-color printing: A printing process which uses cyan, yellow, magenta, and black inks to create a full-color image. Most major magazines use this process.

Gloss: The shine of a paper surface. The higher the gloss of a paper, the more range of density one can accept in the final product. Think of how the photos on the cover of your local newspaper (no gloss) differ from those on a fashion magazine (high gloss).

Gray balance: The combination of cyan, magenta, and yellow inks that produce a neutral gray. Used to check that color separations have the correct balance.

Highlights: The lightest area of an image.

Matte: A soft, smooth finish applied to paper. A matte finish scatters light, and therefore makes things appear dull rather than shiny.

Midtone: The range between highlights and shadows.

Moiré: A distortion on a printed page often caused by the overlapping dot patterns. Most commonly due to scanning and printing an image from another publication. Also can be caused by improper registration of color plates in process printing.

Neutral: A color that has no hue, such as white, black, or gray.

Nonreproducible color: Colors in an original piece of art that cannot be reproduced by the inks available in four-color processing. They are not in the color gamut (range) available in the process.

Press proof: A color proof directly from a press.

Process inks: The inks used in four-color processing. The colors, once again, are cyan, magenta, yellow, and black.

Register: Used as *in register, out of register.* The proper alignment of plates during the printing process produces dots in the correct pattern (see **Rosettes**) which results in the type and images being *in register. Out of register* items appear fuzzy, or have shadows or gaps in color. Good registration creates a crisp, clear image.

Resolution: The ability to see detail in a printed product. Resolution is related to the number of dots in a halftone screen. The more dots, the higher the resolution.

Retouching: Making corrections or alterations to an image either by hand or on the computer. For example, removing a blemish from a model's face.

Rosettes: The dot pattern which is formed when a halftone image is printed in register.

Secondary built colors: The colors created by printing a specific combination of yellow, magenta, cyan, and black inks over one another. Secondary colors in printing include red, green, and blue.

Shadows: The darkest areas of a reproduced image.

Spot color: Non-process ink placed in a specific area. It can be printed in addition to black ink.

Tone: Variation in saturation while the hue (the color) remains the same.

DISTRIBUTION

ne simple rule: The larger your distribution, the more you'll feel forced to compete in a mainstream market. Distribution ranks next only to printing in terms of the annoying practicalities you must deal with to put out a zine. In this chapter, you'll learn which forms of distribution are best for your particular type of zine.

Distribution breaks down into four general methods:

- Free distribution sites.
- Mail order.
- Peddling your zine to stores.
- Distributors.

FREE DROP-OFF POINTS

Free distribution is easy. You go into an establishment frequented by people who might read your zine and ask if you can drop off a stack. Two things to keep in mind:

- Make sure you *ask* if you can drop off your zine, otherwise your zine may end up in the recycling bin before anyone has had the chance to read it. One good idea is to leave a copy with the owner and give him or her a chance to browse through it. After all, she or he is doing you a favor.
- Places that carry numerous free publications may draw crowds of people, but chances are your small zine will get buried under big, floppy, newsprint tabloids, so check these locations and unearth your zines frequently.

MAIL ORDER

The simplest way to deal with mail order is to ask someone to send you a S.A.S.E. with enough postage to cover the cost of mailing your zine. You can also ask for a trade—a copy of their zine, a single, whatever—or for money to help cover your costs. Most zines just let readers know how to order a copy of their zine by placing a small paragraph blurb someplace on the first page of the publication. On rare occasions you can subscribe to zines, and Carla DeSantis, of *ROCKRGRL,* uses the back page of her zine as an order form. By the way, know how you're *never* supposed to send cash in the mail? With zines, you're *always* supposed to send bills (except in the case of ads). They don't bounce, and most people don't run their zine as a business, so money isn't really supposed to change hands in the eyes of Mr. Taxman. When you start legally charging for zines, which can occasionally help you pay *less* taxes, things can get complicated. For example:

- Charging *may* open the door to sales tax. Each state has a separate set of convoluted laws that pertain to taxation of publications. If you live in Oregon, or any other state without sales tax, you're in luck.

- If you live in California and can qualify your fanzine as a newsletter rather than a magazine, you're also off the hook as far as taxes are concerned. If you don't qualify as a newsletter, you have to collect sales tax based on the county rate and pay it to the state either quarterly or annually. In most states, periodicals are tax-free, but you need to check the laws in your particular location. Interstate sales are not taxed, so if you publish in New York and someone in Texas orders your publication, it is tax-exempt for them.

Carla DeSantis started *ROCKRGRL* in 1995 and has had amazing success distributing primarily through mail order. "I had five paid subscribers [when I started]," she laughs. "One father, one good friend, and three people I begged. I was lucky I had some press in the *Los Angeles Times* and I attracted more writers than anything." Two and a half years later, DeSantis has a circulation of 5,000. Despite advertising, it still *costs* her money to produce *ROCKRGRL,* but she has an amazing publication which doesn't bow to the pressure of the marketplace. One important point to remember is that very few people ever break even with their zines. They are a labor of love, or, at the very least, a product of obsession.

RETAIL OUTLETS

If you distribute your publication at retail outlets, they handle the taxes, but in order to survive the dive into the competition for retail space there, chances are your zine will have to look at least somewhat snazzy. Even at retailers sympathetic to zines, space is tight. "As

far as we're concerned, photocopied stuff is being pushed out because with new technology, zines can upgrade pretty quickly," says Ted Gottfried, buyer for See Hear, a fanzine shop and distributor based in New York City. "You can't stop carrying something just because it becomes glossy, especially if it has a readership. The same thing happens at Tower Books and some of the bigger magazine distributors. Let's say they sell a lot of zines; unconsciously, the stuff that looks homemade gets pushed out because there is such a huge number of zines being made. Our retail space is really small, so that happens, and we don't really *want* that to happen."

Retail options for small, photocopied zines do exist, however. They include retail outlets which sell the very thing you're obsessed enough to write about. If you're publishing a zine on cigars, try peddling it to specialty smoke shops. Also, look for hipper retail chains which take zines primarily as a community service. On very rare occasions, one location of a large chain bookstore will have the authority to take zines. "If someone brings something in and says, 'We publish this locally, and we want you to carry it,' usually I'll look at it because I want a sense that we're involved with the community and we know what is going on," says Andru Matthews, periodicals manager at Borders Books in downtown Seattle. "I don't feel like a zine has to be glossy, very few are. With that kind of material, I'm looking for something that people are interested in. Not in terms [of] are they going to sell a lot, but are there people who come in the

> On very rare occasions, one location of a large chain bookstore will have the authority to take zines.

store who think this is cool. If it is something I don't know much about, I'll pass it on to one of my coworkers and go, 'Hey is this cool?' That helps determine my decision, too. I try not to judge on the quality of the material, but rather on the subject matter. Is this about a subject we don't have anything else on? If I am presented with a choice, then I'd carry the good one, but usually that is not the case. They kind of trickle in one at a time and I have to evaluate [each one] on its own merits." Although some chain outlets let people at specific locations add to their corporate list of publications, others require approval through the corporate office.

According to Jeff Smith, publisher of *Feminist Baseball,* there is at least one global chain, Tower Books, that carries zines. "It actually goes to Japan and England, anywhere that there is a Tower," says Smith. "You just send them one and you call them or they call you and they tell you how many they want. Tower seems pretty good. They pay for 60 percent up front. Then, when they give you returns, they pay you for whatever percentage sold minus the 60 percent, which is good, 'cause most people only pay you like three years after they sell them, if they haven't gone out of business."

No matter whether you're dealing with corporate or store policy, some basics always apply:

- Be nice. No one wants to deal with a jerk.
- Be patient. Realize people are busy. Drop off or mail a copy of your best issue to the appropriate person, wait a week, and call to ask if they received your zine and what they think.
- Know how you want to handle returns—Do you want the entire zine returned, the cover only, or just an affidavit which states how many zines were sold?
- Know how you want to be paid. Your options include total payment for zines ordered up front (most people won't do this), partial payment up front, or payment upon return of the zines that have not sold, which is probably what you will end up with, regardless of what you want.

If a retailer or distributor doesn't accept your zine, ask why. They may be able to give you pointers on what needs to be improved in order for them to carry it. Keep in mind, however, that even if you make those changes, distribution is not guaranteed.

Finally, there is something else that is not guaranteed—sales. "You just assume everyone is going to read and love this," says DeSantis. "Unfortunately, that doesn't happen. The problem I have with being on store racks is people can read my 20- to 24-page magazine in 20 minutes—and they do. They read it, it gets dog-eared, and they put it back on the shelf."

Even if a retailer agrees to take your zine, chances are you might get the unsold copies, or at least part of them, back. Most publications are purchased on consignment. The retailer places an order, and you get paid based on what sells. It is important to keep in mind that a retailer may order more than it can sell and, depending on the outlet's returns policy, you may end up without the money *or* your zines.

DISTRIBUTORS

When you decide to use a distributor, you pretty much transform your zine from a hobby into a business, no matter how loosely it is run. You get more circulation but you also open the door to more pressure, not to mention more paperwork! Of course, you can always do exactly what you want with a zine, then throw it out and see what sticks. As zines gain steam, there are organizations and distributors popping up to serve their needs. Most of these groups are still relatively young and you never know how long they'll be around, but the arena is growing. Most people who have dealt specifically with *magazine* distributors have ended up without their zines, without money, and with a head full of frustration.

"Distribution is a really strange thing in its most *acceptable* form, which is, you go through a [magazine] distributor," says DeSantis. "They get clients; it shows up on the racks. The most frustrating thing about distribution is once you send the zines out there, you never get them back. Mostly people will send an affidavit and all you really have is a piece of paper. It's a double-edged sword. You're going to spend money to ship copies, then you're going to split how much you sell with someone else, then you're going to get a piece of paper that tells you how many were returned. So there is a lot of trust involved and a lot of it is with people that are not really trustworthy. There was one very large distributor that sent me a contract. They wanted to take on *ROCKRGRL*. I called them five times, asking how many copies of *ROCKRGRL* they wanted. I couldn't get them to return my phone call, so I'm thinking, what's going to happen when it's time to be paid?"

Jeff Smith, who has been publishing *Feminist Baseball* since 1985, only upped his circulation to 1,000 in 1994, and uses alternative forms of distribution. "The people who distribute *Feminist Baseball* are Tower, Cargo, Revolver U.S.A., and a bunch of record distributors. It's only been the last three years that I've been doing 1,000; before then I was a lot smaller, so I distributed by mail order. We used to go through some magazine distributors, but I didn't have much luck with them. They didn't sell. If they took 50, they'd return 36 and some of them wouldn't return whole copies, which is bad because I can sell them or send them to record companies."

Probably the best and most common way to distribute a zine is through See Hear, a New York–based store and distributor dedicated strictly to zines. Since See Hear understands the culture and purpose of zines, they know how to work with them. "Before we started See Hear," says Ted Gottfried, "which is more than ten years ago, zine distribution was nonexistent. Zines reviewed other zines and you basically bought them through the mail. You ordered them directly from the publishers as an individual. Lots of times we only start with 25 [copies] and see how it goes. A lot of big distributors take hundreds at a time and then, when they don't sell, the zine person is out of luck. They don't realize that just because they sent them a bunch they are not necessarily going to get paid for a bunch—or even see those zines ever again."

> *Probably the best and most common way to distribute a zine is through See Hear...*

MEETING THE DEMANDS OF DISTRIBUTORS

As if sending your zines off into the nether world of a distribution house wasn't bad enough, both that and working with a retailer often cause people to question just why they are publishing in the first place and what they want to achieve. Does the cover look good? Will people read it? Do you care? And *if* you *do* care, just how much are you willing to adjust your concept to capture the attention of those readers? Of course, there are no right answers, but if you want to be picked up by a distributor or hang your zines on the rack of a local retail outlet, here are some hints from people who make the decisions on what to carry, as well as people who have chosen to acknowledge or ignore such advice.

If you choose to access the newsstands, you choose, at least on the surface, to compete with the money and circulation clout of magazines like *Rolling Stone.* Since you're not a mainstream magazine and probably don't want to be, it is important to know what you *are.* Otherwise, people will either write you off, or worse, try to decide for you. "I think it is difficult for a small zine to compete with very store-friendly publications like *Spin* or *Rolling Stone,*" says DeSantis. "They're big, thick, filled with ads, filled with color, and real expensive to produce, but they produce millions of them. For me, content is most critical. Content above everything else—above pictures, above ads—and that is what I concentrate on."

That said, people who deal with zines generally want three things: a good cover, unique content, and someone with whom it won't be too much of a pain in the butt to work. Exactly what is important to whom—and to what extent—varies, of course. On a positive note, there are people like Andru Matthews, the periodicals manager at Borders Books in Seattle, who is in an ideal position. While the corporate offices order mainstream publications, he can enhance the newsstands of the bookstore with his own selections. At the other end of the spectrum is Ted Gottfried, who has dedicated his life to zines. Because he helped develop both a distribution system and a store for zines, he is deluged with more requests than he could possibly service. Gottfried has seen the culture change, and has had to change with it.

DISTRIBUTOR DISCOUNTS

Outside of content and appearance, price, and the publisher's willingness to negotiate payment and provide a discount are other major factors buyers and distributors consider.

The average retail price of a zine usually ranges somewhere between $2 and $5. Obviously, if the zine is extremely large or design-driven, and therefore requires expensive paper, it will cost more. Expect to provide a discount from the newsstand price to the buyer or distributor. That's how they make their profit.

"We look for the right discount off of the cover price so we can resell them to other stores," says Ted Gottfried. "If that is agreeable, then we usually work on consignment. That means when we sell out or when a new issue comes out, we settle up. It's up to [the publishers] how they want to do returns—whole issue, covers, mastheads, or affidavits. There is no rule; it is just whatever gets worked out. As long as everyone is in agreement, I don't care. There is a business-end thing that sometimes gets in the way. They put a cover price on the magazine and then find out it costs them more to print than they thought. We need 55 percent off. We're working on a literary standard of discounting 40 percent to stores, so unless we get 55 percent off, we can't make any money on it. I suggest to people that unless they really know what they are doing, to leave the price off."

So, if a large distributor offers a 40 percent discount to the stores, chances are, when you hit up your local, independently owned bookshop, you'll have to do the same. On the other hand, if someone is nice, he or she often drops it to 25 or 30 percent.

Another thing you'll have to do is negotiate payment. No place pays up front—not for *Vogue,* not for whatever is at the top of the *New York Times* bestseller list, and not for your zine. Once again, how people choose to handle this aspect of their business varies greatly. Some like to purchase things strictly on consignment; others, like Tower, will give you a certain percentage up front. When negotiating a discount, you also need to talk about returns and how they will be handled. Sometimes retailers or distributors will negotiate, other times you are stuck with whatever they offer. Most magazine distributors will only send you an affidavit stating how many of your zines sold, or, at best, the covers of unsold zines for proof. Therefore, if you want the zines back to sell through mail order or to send to advertisers or publicists, it's best to work with someone who specializes in zines. New distributors and retail outlets carrying or dedicated specifically to zines spring up every month. With a little research, you can find which ones are currently in operation. Ask other people who put out zines, or track down some type of zine network or conference, though these also have a short life span.

Several operations, however, have been around for the long haul. Their addresses follow:

Powell's Bookstore
1005 West Burnside
Portland, OR 97209

See Hear
59 East 7th Street
New York, NY 10003

Tower
2601 Del Monte
West Sacramento, CA 95691

PROMOTING YOUR E-ZINE WITH LINKS

 Theoretically, an e-zine is easy to distribute. The only problem is that
without links or a listing in a search engine (a catalog of Web sites), no

one may see your e-zine simply because they do not know it exists.

"As you can imagine, there are millions of pages," says Michael Cox, publisher of the *Music, Coffee, and Baseball* home page. "If you have a paper zine you can put a pile of them in a certain spot and you are guaranteed it will be seen by a certain type of person. The important thing is to get listed and linked from other pages and, hopefully, other pages that people see. Otherwise, you're in a vacuum. There may actually be more work involved in promoting your page than in crafting it."

LIMITATIONS AND POSSIBILITIES

The Internet is often touted as an effective way to reach a large number of people at no cost. In truth, it's an effective way to reach people who are computer literate and fall into the upper-middle-class income bracket or above. On-line services are not free either: You receive a monthly bill. On the other hand, as Michael Cox points out, the Internet provides endless possibilities:

"The Internet is constantly in a state of turmoil. Now it is in a position to be defined not by a particular government agency or people, but by the people who stand to make the most money from it, so it is important that a lot of people do with it what they want or else they'll end up losing it to large interests."

The distribution options for zines change daily. Mail order will probably always be the staple of zine disbursement, and a good review in *Factsheet Five* can cause a boom in orders for any publication. As awareness of and interest in zines increase, distribution houses and specialty stores dedicated specifically to them are becoming more popular, but these are small businesses and they usually struggle to stay in business. For the time being, those who want to read cool zines still have to track them down at obscure outlets or order them through the mail; so word of mouth is still the only way a zine receives any significant recognition.

CHAPTER TEN
DEATH, LOVE, AND TAXES

851—that's the Business Principal or Professional Activity code the IRS has assigned to publishing. If you somehow manage to earn more than a pre-determined amount of money through your zine in a given year, 0851 is the four-digit code required on your tax return. You may never have to worry about that—but, if you decide to distribute your zine at a retailer or accept advertising, it's time to start keeping records. Two manila envelopes for each issue—one for expenses, the other for income—should do the trick. If for some reason your zine takes off and actually starts pulling a large profit, it is time to invest in an accountant, or at least a computerized tax assistance program; but chances are you'll have lots of time to worry about that, if you even *want* your zine to get that big. In this chapter you'll get some guidelines for when and if you need to start worrying about taxes as well as some guidelines for choosing a Schedule SE or C-EZ at tax time.

There are those who put out zines that might ignore the tax question altogether. It comes into play primarily when zines start interacting with legitimate businesses, such as retailers, distributors, and people who purchase advertising from you. They keep books, so *you* have to—just in case Mr. Taxman decides to check.

Note that, if your zine is sold through the mail, you may also have to charge state sales tax. As mentioned in Chapter 9, interstate sales are not taxable and intrastate (within-state) publication sales are not taxable in most states. Whether or not you decide to charge sales tax to pass on to the state capitol on your mail-order transactions, it never hurts to keep records for backup. If your zine is distributed at retail outlets, they take care of taxes. Tax laws change frequently, and you can find out whether or not you are required to pay them on in-state mail order zine sales by calling your State Department of Commerce.

SE AND C-EZ

Income taxes are a different bailiwick altogether. First off, if you earn less than a specified amount (again, you'll have to check that figure each year, but for example purposes, we'll use $400, the amount indicated by the IRS at the time this book was published), it can go on the line of your 1040 form dedicated to "other income," including that derived from hobbies. Those who earn more than the annually specified amount might have to fill out a schedule SE and C or, more than likely, Short Schedule SE and C-EZ.

Schedule SE, which you file as an addition to a 1040, is for self-employment tax. Schedule C, which you file as an adjunct to Schedule SE (charming, isn't it?), is for a business you operate or a sole proprietorship you have. In the words of the IRS: "An activity qualifies as a business if your primary purpose for engaging in the activity is for income or profit and you are involved in the activity with continuity and regularity. For example, a sporadic activity or a hobby does not qualify as a business." On the other hand, the phrase "income from the retail sales of newspapers and magazines if you were 18 or older and kept the profits" is included under the subhead "Other Income and Losses Included in Net Earnings From Self-Employment."

Use the "hobbies, etc." line on the 1040 form whenever possible. The self-employment tax calculated on the SE Schedule may result in a lower rate than that charged on the 1040 form. On that condescending "hobby" line, the IRS assesses your income tax, while, on the SE Schedule, you also pay your own Social Security and Medicare tax. However, using Schedule SE may benefit you if you purchase equipment to put out a zine or spend a great deal on printing. It is necessary to keep in mind that the IRS is strict in what it considers "deductible," especially when it comes to media and art. Many home computers don't qualify for deduction since the government assumes people use them for personal purposes. To see whether using Schedule SE would be to your benefit, pick up the IRS publication on self-employment tax. It can provide the details for your particular situation. And no matter what forms you use, it's necessary to keep records for at least three years after the date you file or pay taxes, whichever comes later.

SE OPTIONAL

Although most zines might not earn a profit, it's still important to keep records. You have to file an SE form if you *earn* (gross) more than a specific amount. It has nothing to do with *profit*. The amount you earn includes all incoming funds, while profit (net) is the amount you have left from those incoming funds once you pay all your expenses. Additionally, the minimum amount you can earn without paying taxes is small, so if you do business with other people (distributors, vendors, advertisers) and you earn anything more than $100, it is best to check.

> *The amount you earn includes all incoming funds, while profit (net) is the amount you have left from those incoming funds once you pay all your expenses.*

If you've been publishing a zine for several years, there is also a chance that you can pay reduced taxes by using the SE Optional Method. To qualify, you have to meet the following criteria:

- Your net (after expenses) self-employment income (from your zine and all other sources) must be less than a specific amount; at the time of this publication, it was $1,733.
- Your self-employment income profits (income minus expenses) must be less than a specified percent of the income you earn through self-employment (72.189 percent at time of publishing). For example: If you earn $1,000 from your zine in a particular year, it must cost you at least $278 to produce your zine. The equation is as follows:
  —Step One: Income − expenses = profit.
  —Step Two: Profit ÷ income ≤ than the amount specified by the IRS.
  The numbers above were determined as follows:
  —Income ($1,000) − expenses ($828) = profit ($172).
  —Profit ($172) ÷ income ($1,000) ≤ specified amount (in this case 17.2 percent).
- You must have produced your zine (or have been in some other way regularly self-employed) in at least two of the three previous

tax years. In other words, you have to have filed an SE form in at least two of the last three years.

- You can't previously have taken advantage of this method more than four times.

This option is then divided into two categories: those earning above, or below, yet another specified amount. Once again, we'll use the figure indicated by the IRS at publication time ($2,400). Those who earn less than the specified amount can report two-thirds of the money earned from a zine (and any other self-employment) rather than the total amount. You may save 33 percent this way. Those who earn more than the specified figure, and meet all the four criteria

---

SCHEDULE C-EZ
(Form 1040)

Department of the Treasury
Internal Revenue Service   (O)

Net Profit From Business
(Sole Proprietorship)
▶ Partnerships, joint ventures, etc., must file Form 1065.
▶ Attach to Form 1040 or Form 1041. ▶ See instructions on back.

OMB No. 1545-0074

1995

Attachment
Sequence No. **09A**

Name of proprietor

Social security number (SSN)

Part I   **General Information**

**You May Use
This Schedule
Only If You:**

- Had gross receipts from your business of $25,000 or less.
- Had business expenses of $2,000 or less.
- Use the cash method of accounting.
- Did not have an inventory at any time during the year.
- Did not have a net loss from your business.
- Had only one business as a sole proprietor.

And You:

- Had no employees during the year.
- Are not required to file **Form 4562**, Depreciation and Amortization, for this business. See the instructions for Schedule C, line 13, on page C-3 to find out if you must file.
- Do not deduct expenses for business use of your home.
- Do not have prior year unallowed passive activity losses from this business.

A Principal business or profession, including product or service
FANZINE PUBLISHER

B Enter principal business code (see page C-6) ▶ |0|8|5|1|

C Business name. If no separate business name, leave blank.
Zine Inc.

D Employer ID number (EIN), if any
6:8|6|6|6|6|6

E Business address (including suite or room no.). Address not required if same as on Form 1040, page 1.
1666 69 St SW
City, town or post office, state, and ZIP code
Seattle WA 9802

Part II   **Figure Your Net Profit**

1	**Gross receipts.** If more than $25,000, you **must** use Schedule C. **Caution:** If this income was reported to you on Form W-2 and the "Statutory employee" box on that form was checked, see **Statutory Employees** in the instructions for Schedule C, line 1, on page C-2 and check here . . . . ▶ ☐	**1**	2000 00
2	**Total expenses.** If more than $2,000, you **must** use Schedule C. See instructions	**2**	500 00
3	**Net profit.** Subtract line 2 from line 1. If less than zero, you **must** use Schedule C. Enter on **Form 1040, line 12,** and ALSO on **Schedule SE, line 2.** (Statutory employees **do not** report this amount on Schedule SE, line 2. Estates and trusts, enter on Form 1041, line 3.)	**3**	1500 00

Part III   **Information on Your Vehicle.** Complete this part ONLY if you are claiming car or truck expenses on line 2.

4 When did you place your vehicle in service for business purposes? (month, day, year) ▶ 6 / 6 / 96

5 Of the total number of miles you drove your vehicle during 1995, enter the number of miles you used your vehicle for:

a Business 500   **b** Commuting 20,000   **c** Other

6 Do you (or your spouse) have another vehicle available for personal use? . . . . ☐ Yes ☒ No

7 Was your vehicle available for use during off-duty hours? . . . . ☒ Yes ☐ No

8a Do you have evidence to support your deduction? . . . . ☒ Yes ☐ No

b If "Yes," is the evidence written? . . . . ☒ Yes ☐ No

For Paperwork Reduction Act Notice, see Form 1040 instructions.   Cat. No. 14374D   Schedule C-EZ (Form 1040) 1995

**Front of Schedule C-EZ
(Form 1040), Net Profit From Business**

mentioned above, may report a lesser amount, once again determined by the IRS (get the self-employment publication for that year to find the specific amount).

DEDUCTIONS

If you decide, or rather, if the government decides, that you should file the SE Schedule, the receipts and records you've stashed in those manila envelopes may significantly reduce your taxes. Without them, you may find yourself losing more to the government in taxes than you did while producing your zine! Make sure to track and keep billings and receipts for the following:

- Computer equipment and programs.
- Printing.
- Supplies, including paper, books, magazines, and miscellaneous office goodies.
- Travel (although if you claim you use your personal car for business purposes, your insurance might go up).
- Phone bills, although you need to keep in mind the phone company may charge higher rates if they think you have a "business line."
- Office space. If your operation and home meet the right criteria, you may even be able to deduct part of your rent.

If your zine for some reason gets huge, grows out of proportion, and enters that nebulous world where people start to think of it as a magazine, it might be wise to hire an accountant at tax time, as he or she knows exactly how and what things to deduct legally, and can amortize high-cost items to your benefit. If you actually manage to make a living from your zine—it's rare but a few people have done it—consider getting a tax number and business license. They may provide a lot more money-saving options.

If you want to stay small, it's simple—ignore demand. Even if you do decide to run your publication like a business, chances are you won't pull a profit, but it will help out financially in the short run. Or you can take *ROCKRGRL* Carla DeSantis' advice: "Anyone who has a zine is more often than not going to be operating in the red," she says. "You need to keep really good records. Save your receipts for everything, but remember you can only operate a certain number of years at a loss before the government will no longer let you write it off. If someone's going to do this, they really have to look at it as a labor of love, first and foremost."

NUMBERS FOR YOUR FRIENDS AT THE IRS

For Tax Forms: 1-800-TAX-FORMS

TELE-TAX

These numbers provide prerecorded information on a variety of topics, including help for small businesses, recordkeeping, sole proprietorships, business use of your home, and business use of a car. The toll free number is 1-800-829-4477 or, if you're in one of several selected major metropolitan areas, as follows:

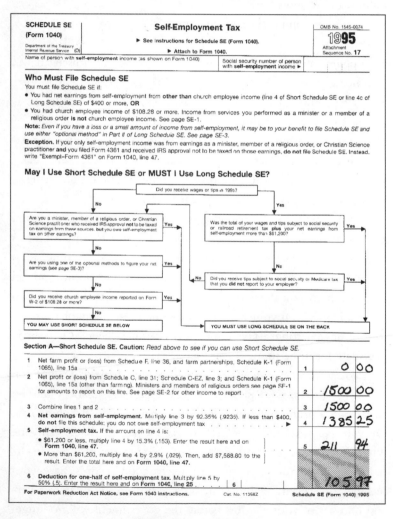

Front of Schedule SE (Form 1040), Self-Employment Tax

Phoenix, AZ: (602) 640-3933

Oakland, CA: (510) 839-4245

Denver, CO: (303) 592-1118

District of Columbia: (202) 628-2929

Atlanta, GA: (404) 331-6572

Chicago, IL: (312) 886-9614

Springfield, IL: (217) 789-0489

Indianapolis, IN: (317) 631-1010

Des Moines, IA: (515) 284-7454

Boston, MA: (617) 536-0709

Schedule SE (Form 1040) 1995		Attachment Sequence No **17**	Page **2**
Name of person with **self-employment** income (as shown on Form 1040)		Social security number of person with self-employment income ▶	

Section B—Long Schedule SE

Part I Self-Employment Tax

Note: If your only income subject to self-employment tax is **church employee income,** skip lines 1 through 4b. Enter -0- on line 4c and go to line 5a. Income from services you performed as a minister or a member of a religious order is **not** church employee income. See page SE-1.

A If you are a minister, member of a religious order, or Christian Science practitioner **and** you filed Form 4361, but you had $400 or more of **other** net earnings from self-employment, check here and continue with Part I . . . . ▶ ☐

1 Net farm profit or (loss) from Schedule F, line 36, and farm partnerships, Schedule K-1 (Form 1065), line 15a. **Note:** Skip this line if you use the farm optional method. See page SE-3 — **1**

2 Net profit or (loss) from Schedule C, line 31; Schedule C-EZ, line 3; and Schedule K-1 (Form 1065), line 15a (other than farming). Ministers and members of religious orders see page SE-1 for amounts to report on this line. See page SE-2 for other income to report. **Note:** Skip this line if you use the nonfarm optional method. See page SE-3 — **2**

3 Combine lines 1 and 2 . . . . **3**

4a If line 3 is more than zero, multiply line 3 by 92.35% (.9235). Otherwise, enter amount from line 3 — **4a**

b If you elected one or both of the optional methods, enter the total of lines 15 and 17 here . . — **4b**

c Combine lines 4a and 4b. If less than $400, **do not** file this schedule; you do not owe self-employment tax. **Exception.** If less than $400 and you had **church employee income,** enter -0- and continue ▶ **4c**

5a Enter your **church employee income** from Form W-2. **Caution:** See page SE-1 for definition of church employee income . . . **5a** — **5b**

b Multiply line 5a by 92.35% (.9235). If less than $100, enter -0- **5b**

6 **Net earnings from self-employment.** Add lines 4c and 5b **6**

7 Maximum amount of combined wages and self-employment earnings subject to social security tax or the 6.2% portion of the 7.65% railroad retirement (tier 1) tax for 1995 . . . . **7** | 61,200 | 00

8a Total social security wages and tips (total of boxes 3 and 7 on Form(s) W-2) and railroad retirement (tier 1) compensation **8a**

b Unreported tips subject to social security tax (from Form 4137, line 9) **8b**

c Add lines 8a and 8b **8c**

9 Subtract line 8c from line 7. If zero or less, enter -0- here and on line 10 and go to line 11 . ▶ **9**

10 Multiply the **smaller** of line 6 or line 9 by 12.4% (.124) **10**

11 Multiply line 6 by 2.9% (.029) **11**

12 **Self-employment tax.** Add lines 10 and 11. Enter here and on **Form 1040, line 47** . . . **12**

13 **Deduction for one-half of self-employment tax.** Multiply line 12 by 50% (.5). Enter the result here and on **Form 1040, line 25** **13**

Part II Optional Methods To Figure Net Earnings (See page SE-3.)

Farm Optional Method. You may use this method **only if:**
• Your gross farm income[1] was not more than $2,400, **or**
• Your gross farm income[1] was more than $2,400 and your net farm profits[2] were less than $1,733.

14 Maximum income for optional methods . . . . **14** | 1,600 | 00

15 Enter the **smaller** of: two-thirds (⅔) of gross farm income[1] (not less than zero) **or** $1,600. Also, include this amount on line 4b above **15**

Nonfarm Optional Method. You may use this method **only if:**
• Your net nonfarm profits[3] were less than $1,733 and also less than 72.189% of your gross nonfarm income,[4] **and**
• You had net earnings from self-employment of at least $400 in 2 of the prior 3 years.
Caution: You may use this method no more than five times.

16 Subtract line 15 from line 14 . . . . **16**

17 Enter the **smaller** of: two-thirds (⅔) of gross nonfarm income[4] (not less than zero) **or** the amount on line 16. Also, include this amount on line 4b above **17**

[1]From Schedule F, line 11, and Schedule K-1 (Form 1065), line 15b. [3]From Schedule C, line 31; Schedule C-EZ, line 3; and Schedule K-1 (Form 1065), line 15a.
[2]From Schedule F, line 36, and Schedule K-1 (Form 1065), line 15a. [4]From Schedule C, line 7; Schedule C-EZ, line 1; and Schedule K-1 (Form 1065), line 15c.

Printed on recycled paper   U.S. Government Printing Office: 1995 — 389-220

**Back of Schedule SE
(Form 1040), Self-Employment Tax**

Baltimore, MD: (410) 244-7306

Detroit, MI: (313) 961-4282

Minneapolis, MN: (612) 644-7748

St. Paul, MN: (612) 644-7748

St. Louis, MO: (314) 241-4700

Omaha, NE: (402) 221-3324

Buffalo, NY: (716) 685-5533

Cincinnati, OH: (513) 421-0329

Cleveland, OH: (216) 522-3037

Portland, OR: (503) 294-5363

Philadelphia, PA: (215) 627-1040

Pittsburgh, PA: (412) 261-1040

Nashville, TN: (615) 781-5040

Dallas, TX: (214) 767-1792

Houston, TX: (713) 541-3400

Richmond, VA: (804) 783-1569

Seattle, WA: (206) 343-7221

Milwaukee, WI: (414) 273-8100

Tax Help Lines: 1-800-829-1040

(or use the local numbers below)

Tax Help Lines provide personalized service. In other words, you get to ask a person a question versus receiving the prerecorded information available on the Tele-Tax Lines.

Phoenix, AZ: (602) 640-3930

Oakland, CA: (510) 839-1040

Denver, CO: (303) 825-7041

Jacksonville, FL: (904) 354-1760

Atlanta, GA: (404) 522-0050

Indianapolis, IN: (317) 226-5477

Boston, MA: (617) 536-1040

Baltimore, MD: (410) 962-2590

Detroit, MI: (313) 237-0800

Minneapolis, MN: (612) 644-7515

St. Paul, MN: (612) 644-7515

St. Louis, MO: (314) 342-1040

Buffalo, NY: (716) 685-5432

Cincinnati, OH: (513) 621-6281

Cleveland, OH: (216) 522-3000

Portland, OR: (503) 221-3960

Philadelphia, PA: (215) 574-9900

Pittsburgh, PA: (412) 281-0112

Nashville, TN: (615) 834-9005

Dallas, TX: (214) 742-2440

Houston, TX: (713) 541-0440

Richmond, VA: (804) 689-5000

Seattle, WA: (206) 442-1040

Taxes are no fun, but it's important to pay unless you choose t refrain for political reasons. The bottom line is that there's one sir ple rule to reduce the amount of taxes you pay: Keep good reco You can deduct most of your costs, and a publisher can most tainly deduct his or her major costs—printing. Those who good records will find they pay minimal taxes, if any at all.

CHAPTER ELEVEN
SELLING OUT

t's only been in the past ten years that zines have seen stores or distributors devoted to them. "It's really new," says Ted Gottfried, buyer for See Hear. "That's what is great about zines. They are idealistic, but this idea that you are going to start one and it's going to be your living is totally crazy. There is just no way. It comes down to, 'Why publish?' That is truly what zines are about: People who *have* to write; people who have to publish for some reason. People have lots of different reasons for that, but if they're going into it with the idea that they're going to be a successful publisher, it's nuts. Some zines have had success, crossed over, and are a living for people—but not too many."

So you can try to sell out, but no one's buying. OK, that's not completely true. People are buying, although the nature of zines pretty much defines them as not-for-profit publications. That is the primary outward difference that remains—and always will—between fanzines and magazines. From the cover, you might not be able to distinguish between a highly produced fanzine and a low-end magazine. The difference lies in the pages, both in attitude and style. If your purpose is to make a living from publishing, start a magazine; or better yet, go to work for one. It requires less capital.

Those who produce magazines have to worry about circulation and who consumes the publication. They conduct studies to find out what age group and gender read their publication as well as what those people buy and do in their spare time. Drink beer? Shop for auto parts? Fight acne? Who cares? The major advertisers that purchase scads of high-cost column inches and keep large publications in business do. That's what encourages people to advertise. Since they are in business primarily to pull a profit, magazines like that often try to appeal either to the most general readership possible or to a specific niche of people that no one else is pandering to at the moment. It increases revenue from circulation and advertising. The result? Magazines have to monitor what they print in order to keep their readers happy and the bucks rolling in. This is not necessarily a *bad*

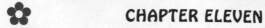

thing. Magazines supply a service. They also provide jobs that are a heck of lot more interesting than slinging hash at the local deli. Many an independent publisher has gone on to edit or freelance for a magazine. Additionally, a lot of magazine editors publish a zine so they can write about their current obsession without having to worry about whether the topic interests or offends their readership.

Fanzines stand in direct opposition to the commercial aspects of magazines. They are an act of guerrilla publishing. As always, there's a cost for contradicting commercial standards, not to mention keeping yourself amused for hours on end. In the case of fanzines, it's the money to keep a publication afloat. Advertising and charging for an issue can help defray the costs of publishing, but rarely will they cover them. A zine is rarely so bland or general that it attracts enough readers to exceed its production cost, let alone pay the rent and fill the stomach of the person who puts it out. On the other hand, independent publishers can write about whatever odd topic has come to roost in their brain at the moment.

The only thing one can truly define as "selling out" is betraying your own standards. That's different for everybody: for some it means not accepting advertising; for others it translates to not bending to a distributor's demand that a zine have a glossy or color cover; for almost everyone, it means publishing a zine that covers what he or she likes, or wishes to comment on, and *nothing else.*

With mass-media outlets becoming part of large publishing and broadcast empires, the role of zines is changing. People want alternatives and zines fill the void. A look at one of zine's older cousins, independent record labels, provides a glimpse into the struggles and options the future may hold for independent publishers. In the '70s, music was dished out to the masses much like the print and broadcast media are today. Few other options existed, so people interested in alternatives created their own. Most of those labels remained small and put out a few records; many of them disappeared as people lost interest; some still exist on a small level; and others have grown into large counterculture businesses such as Epitaph or merged with major labels as Sub Pop did. Many of those same options will inevitably come to exist in the world of publishing for zines.

Sub Pop started as a small, independent label dedicated to putting out bands from the Northwest. Their records sold only to people who already knew and cared about the groups; the artists were

Phoenix, AZ: (602) 640–3933

Oakland, CA: (510) 839–4245

Denver, CO: (303) 592–1118

District of Columbia: (202) 628–2929

Atlanta, GA: (404) 331–6572

Chicago, IL: (312) 886–9614

Springfield, IL: (217) 789–0489

Indianapolis, IN: (317) 631–1010

Des Moines, IA: (515) 284–7454

Boston, MA: (617) 536–0709

Schedule SE (Form 1040) 1995   Attachment Sequence No **17**   Page **2**

Name of person with **self-employment** income (as shown on Form 1040) | Social security number of person with **self-employment** income ▶

Section B—Long Schedule SE

Part I   **Self-Employment Tax**

Note: *If your only income subject to self-employment tax is church employee income, skip lines 1 through 4b. Enter -0- on line 4c and go to line 5a. Income from services you performed as a minister or a member of a religious order is not church employee income. See page SE-1.*

A   If you are a minister, member of a religious order, or Christian Science practitioner **and** you filed Form 4361, but you had $400 or more of **other** net earnings from self-employment, check here and continue with Part I . . . . . ▶ ☐

1   Net farm profit or (loss) from Schedule F, line 36, and farm partnerships, Schedule K-1 (Form 1065), line 15a. **Note:** *Skip this line if you use the farm optional method. See page SE-3*   **1**

2   Net profit or (loss) from Schedule C, line 31; Schedule C-EZ, line 3; and Schedule K-1 (Form 1065), line 15a (other than farming). Ministers and members of religious orders see page SE-1 for amounts to report on this line. See page SE-2 for other income to report. **Note:** *Skip this line if you use the nonfarm optional method. See page SE-3.*   **2**

3   Combine lines 1 and 2 . . . .   **3**

4a   If line 3 is more than zero, multiply line 3 by 92.35% (.9235). Otherwise, enter amount from line 3   **4a**

   b   If you elected one or both of the optional methods, enter the total of lines 15 and 17 here . .   **4b**

   c   Combine lines 4a and 4b. If less than $400, **do not** file this schedule; you do not owe self-employment tax. **Exception.** If less than $400 and you had **church employee income,** enter -0- and continue ▶   **4c**

5a   Enter your **church employee income** from Form W-2. **Caution:** *See page SE-1 for definition of church employee income* . . | **5a**

   b   Multiply line 5a by 92.35% (.9235). If less than $100, enter -0- **5b**

6   **Net earnings from self-employment.** Add lines 4c and 5b **6**

7   Maximum amount of combined wages and self-employment earnings subject to social security tax or the 6.2% portion of the 7.65% railroad retirement (tier 1) tax for 1995 . . . . .   **7**   61,200 | 00

8a   Total social security wages and tips (total of boxes 3 and 7 on Form(s) W-2) and railroad retirement (tier 1) compensation . . . . . | **8a**

   b   Unreported tips subject to social security tax (from Form 4137, line 9) | **8b**

   c   Add lines 8a and 8b **8c**

9   Subtract line 8c from line 7. If zero or less, enter -0- here and on line 10 and go to line 11 ▶   **9**

10   Multiply the **smaller** of line 6 or line 9 by 12.4% (.124) **10**

11   Multiply line 6 by 2.9% (.029). **11**

12   **Self-employment tax.** Add lines 10 and 11. Enter here and on **Form 1040, line 47** **12**

13   **Deduction for one-half of self-employment tax.** Multiply line 12 by 50% (.5). Enter the result here and on **Form 1040, line 26** . . . . | **13**

Part II   **Optional Methods To Figure Net Earnings** (See page SE-3.)

Farm Optional Method. You may use this method only if:
• Your gross farm income[1] was not more than $2,400, **or**
• Your gross farm income was more than $2,400 and your net farm profits[2] were less than $1,733.

14   Maximum income for optional methods . . . .   **14**   1,600 | 00

15   Enter the **smaller** of: two-thirds (⅔) of gross farm income[1] (not less than zero) **or** $1,600. Also, include this amount on line 4b above **15**

Nonfarm Optional Method. You may use this method **only** if:
• Your net nonfarm profits[3] were less than $1,733 and also less than 72.189% of your gross nonfarm income,[4] **and**
• You had net earnings from self-employment of at least $400 in 2 of the prior 3 years.
Caution: *You[4] may use this method no more than five times.*

16   Subtract line 15 from line 14 . . . .   **16**

17   Enter the **smaller** of: two-thirds (⅔) of gross nonfarm income[4] (not less than zero) **or** the amount on line 16. Also, include this amount on line 4b above **17**

[1] From Schedule F, line 11, and Schedule K-1 (Form 1065), line 15b.   [3] From Schedule C, line 31; Schedule C-EZ, line 3; and Schedule K-1 (Form 1065), line 15a.
[2] From Schedule F, line 36, and Schedule K-1 (Form 1065), line 15a.   [4] From Schedule C, line 7; Schedule C-EZ, line 1; and Schedule K-1 (Form 1065), line 15c.

    ♻   Printed on recycled paper   *U.S. Government Printing Office: 1995 — 389-220

**Back of Schedule SE
(Form 1040), Self-Employment Tax**

Baltimore, MD: (410) 244-7306

Detroit, MI: (313) 961-4282

Minneapolis, MN: (612) 644-7748

St. Paul, MN: (612) 644-7748

St. Louis, MO: (314) 241-4700

Omaha, NE: (402) 221-3324

Buffalo, NY: (716) 685-5533

Cincinnati, OH: (513) 421-0329

Cleveland, OH: (216) 522-3037

Portland, OR: (503) 294-5363

Philadelphia, PA: (215) 627-1040

Pittsburgh, PA: (412) 261-1040

Nashville, TN: (615) 781-5040

Dallas, TX: (214) 767-1792

Houston, TX: (713) 541-3400

Richmond, VA: (804) 783-1569

Seattle, WA: (206) 343-7221

Milwaukee, WI: (414) 273-8100

Tax Help Lines: 1-800-829-1040
(or use the local numbers below)

Tax Help Lines provide personalized service. In other words, you get to ask a person a question versus receiving the prerecorded information available on the Tele-Tax Lines.

Phoenix, AZ: (602) 640-3930

Oakland, CA: (510) 839-1040

Denver, CO: (303) 825-7041

Jacksonville, FL: (904) 354-1760

Atlanta, GA: (404) 522-0050

Indianapolis, IN: (317) 226-5477

Boston, MA: (617) 536-1040

Baltimore, MD: (410) 962-2590

Detroit, MI: (313) 237-0800

Minneapolis, MN: (612) 644-7515

St. Paul, MN: (612) 644-7515

St. Louis, MO: (314) 342-1040

Buffalo, NY: (716) 685-5432

Cincinnati, OH: (513) 621-6281

Cleveland, OH: (216) 522-3000

Portland, OR: (503) 221-3960

Philadelphia, PA: (215) 574-9900

Pittsburgh, PA: (412) 281-0112

Nashville, TN: (615) 834-9005

Dallas, TX: (214) 742-2440

Houston, TX: (713) 541-0440

Richmond, VA: (804) 689-5000

Seattle, WA: (206) 442-1040

Taxes are no fun, but it's important to pay unless you choose to refrain for political reasons. The bottom line is that there's one simple rule to reduce the amount of taxes you pay: Keep good records. You can deduct most of your costs, and a publisher can most certainly deduct his or her major costs—printing. Those who keep good records will find they pay minimal taxes, if any at all.

CHAPTER ELEVEN
SELLING OUT

t's only been in the past ten years that zines have seen stores or distributors devoted to them. "It's really new," says Ted Gottfried, buyer for See Hear. "That's what is great about zines. They are idealistic, but this idea that you are going to start one and it's going to be your living is totally crazy. There is just no way. It comes down to, 'Why publish?' That is truly what zines are about: People who *have* to write; people who have to publish for some reason. People have lots of different reasons for that, but if they're going into it with the idea that they're going to be a successful publisher, it's nuts. Some zines have had success, crossed over, and are a living for people—but not too many."

So you can try to sell out, but no one's buying. OK, that's not completely true. People are buying, although the nature of zines pretty much defines them as not-for-profit publications. That is the primary outward difference that remains—and always will—between fanzines and magazines. From the cover, you might not be able to distinguish between a highly produced fanzine and a low-end magazine. The difference lies in the pages, both in attitude and style. If your purpose is to make a living from publishing, start a magazine; or better yet, go to work for one. It requires less capital.

Those who produce magazines have to worry about circulation and who consumes the publication. They conduct studies to find out what age group and gender read their publication as well as what those people buy and do in their spare time. Drink beer? Shop for auto parts? Fight acne? Who cares? The major advertisers that purchase scads of high-cost column inches and keep large publications in business do. That's what encourages people to advertise. Since they are in business primarily to pull a profit, magazines like that often try to appeal either to the most general readership possible or to a specific niche of people that no one else is pandering to at the moment. It increases revenue from circulation and advertising. The result? Magazines have to monitor what they print in order to keep their readers happy and the bucks rolling in. This is not necessarily a *bad* thing. Magazines supply a service. They also provide jobs that are a heck of lot more interesting than slinging hash at the local deli. Many an independent publisher has gone on to edit or freelance for a magazine. Additionally, a lot of magazine editors publish a zine so they can write about their current obsession without having to worry about whether the topic interests or offends their readership.

Fanzines stand in direct opposition to the commercial aspects of magazines. They are an act of guerrilla publishing. As always, there's a cost for contradicting commercial standards, not to mention keeping yourself amused for hours on end. In the case of fanzines, it's the money to keep a publication afloat. Advertising and charging for an issue can help defray the costs of publishing, but rarely will they cover them. A zine is rarely so bland or general that it attracts enough readers to exceed its production cost, let alone pay the rent and fill the stomach of the person who puts it out. On the other hand, independent publishers can write about whatever odd topic has come to roost in their brain at the moment.

The only thing one can truly define as "selling out" is betraying your own standards. That's different for everybody: for some it means not accepting advertising; for others it translates to not bending to a distributor's demand that a zine have a glossy or color cover; for almost everyone, it means publishing a zine that covers what he or she likes, or wishes to comment on, and *nothing else.*

With mass-media outlets becoming part of large publishing and broadcast empires, the role of zines is changing. People want alternatives and zines fill the void. A look at one of zine's older cousins, independent record labels, provides a glimpse into the struggles and options the future may hold for independent publishers. In the '70s, music was dished out to the masses much like the print and broadcast media are today. Few other options existed, so people interested in alternatives created their own. Most of those labels remained small and put out a few records; many of them disappeared as people lost interest; some still exist on a small level; and others have grown into large counterculture businesses such as Epitaph or merged with major labels as Sub Pop did. Many of those same options will inevitably come to exist in the world of publishing for zines.

Sub Pop started as a small, independent label dedicated to putting out bands from the Northwest. Their records sold only to people who already knew and cared about the groups; the artists were obscure and profit margins nonexistent. Eventually, the owners decided they were sitting on a heap of talent that the world was ready to hear, and Sub Pop proceeded to make the label a commercial venture. To announce this, they adopted the blatant slogan "World Domination." In addition to providing a clever marketing gimmick, it signified a change in the label's intent. In a similar way, an independent publisher who switches from producing a zine strictly for the purposes of communication and amusement to creating a magazine for both commercial and communicative reasons should consider clarifying their ambition as well. If you want to produce a magazine, say so. You'll be

Fanzines stand in direct opposition to the commercial aspects of magazines.

more likely to receive the advertising you crave and it will keep the role of zines clear.

The void left by media conglomerates is being filled both by zines and by independently published magazines like *Option, Utne Reader,* and *Ms.* In fact, *Ms* does not accept advertising, and so one could almost define it as a zine. The distinctions are blurred. The difference lies in *intent.* Carla DeSantis, publisher of *ROCKRGRL,* a zine dedicated to female musicians, sees her role in publishing as that of advocate rather than critic or journalist. In addition to running a zine with a circulation of 5,000, DeSantis has well-known female journalists contributing to her zine (sans monetary compensation) and has helped put a serious dent in the boys club of the music industry. Yet DeSantis has yet to earn a profit from her efforts. Obviously, that's not her primary purpose. She would prefer that her zine be totally subscription-driven, but she does accept advertising to reduce her losses.

"Early on, people said to me, 'You could be like *Option* or *Rolling Stone,'*" says DeSantis. "Those are not my aspirations. My biggest dream is to have women tell me that after they read an article they wrote ten songs. My biggest goal is *not* to have Levi's or Virginia Slims ads."

The transitions taking place in today's media mean there are immense gaps for various types of self-publishing to fill. You can do anything you want. It's all a matter of balancing: Defray the costs or